Wild Woman

Wild Woman

A FOOTNOTE, THE DESERT, AND MY QUEST FOR AN ELUSIVE SAINT

AMY FRYKHOLM

Broadleaf Books
Minneapolis

WILD WOMAN
A Footnote, the Desert, and My Quest for an Elusive Saint

Cover art: Martha Davies / Getty Images

Print ISBN: 978-1-5064-7185-3
eBook ISBN: 978-1-5064-7186-0

Printed in Canada

For the stranger within and without who needs welcome

CONTENTS

CONTENTS

MEDITERRANEAN SEA

ALEXANDRIA

EGYPT

THE NILE

MONASTERY OF
ST. ANTHONY

RED SEA

ASWAN

NUBIA

IN

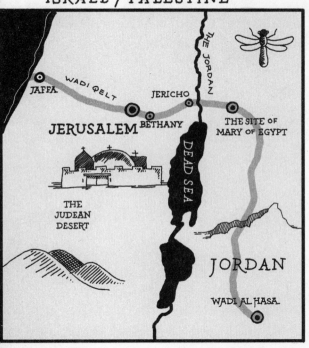

ISRAEL / PALESTINE

THE JORDAN

JAFFA
WADI QELT
JERICHO
JERUSALEM
BETHANY
THE SITE OF
MARY OF EGYPT

DEAD SEA

THE
JUDEAN
DESERT

JORDAN

WADI AL HASA

PREFACE

FOOTNOTE TO HISTORY

If you have a deep scar, that is a door, if you have an old, old story, that is a door. If you love the sky and the water so much that you almost cannot bear it, that is a door. If you yearn for a deeper life, a full life, a sane life, that is a door.
  —Clarissa Pinkola Estés, *Women Who Run with the Wolves*

I came to this story looking for a footnote*—a fact that seems ironic given what a faint footprint I started following. I was in the Norlin Library on the campus of the University of Colorado at Boulder. Outside, the shadow on the sundial near the library door swept along as usual. But inside, there might as well not have been time. I was finishing a manuscript for a book, and I was in the midst of the tedious process of verifying page numbers and publishers and dates for the footnotes, tracking down books whose ideas I had long since devoured and digested.

After working all morning, I found myself at midday hungry and wandering among the stacks. I suppose I needed a lunch break but was reluctant to take it with so many footnotes still to go. I cannot account for the flight of the book—unattractive, dusty—into my hands. I was

---

* I first wrote this entire book without footnotes or endnotes, and you may want to read it that way as well. I have included notes along the way to offer more of what I found in my exploration of Mary of Egypt—and because I am always grateful when other writers leave me maps to follow.

not looking for it. Having spent my morning with the tiniest of the tiny print, more print should not have been interesting. The book was called *Holy Women of Byzantium: Ten Saints' Lives in English Translation*. I sat down on the thin carpet, leaned back against other volumes, opened the book at random—directly to the story of St. Mary of Egypt, of whom I had never heard—and began to read.

Always an impatient reader, I skipped the introduction to her story, the background and context offered by the translator of the seventh-century text. I also skipped, instinctively, the opening paragraphs: "It is good to keep close the secrets of a king . . ."

"Who cares?" I may or may not have whispered aloud. For me, the story began at a section marked 10. I leafed through the pages as if I knew what I was looking for: "While he was chanting psalms and looking up to heaven with an alert eye, he saw the shadowy illusion of a human body appear to the right of where he was standing and performing the prayers at the sixth hour." The rest I read hungrily to the end. I took the book with me to lunch, and while I ate at a deli in the U District, I took out a piece of paper and a pencil and began to eliminate all the words in Maria Kouli's translation that my mind's eye saw as unnecessary:

Chanting psalms
at the sixth hour

he saw a shadow

a body as if
scorched by the sun

hair sparse and wooly white

he ran weeping
until both came

to a streambed
that had left its trace

How could a torrent
appear in that land?

I am no ghost, she said,
but altogether earth and ashes and flesh.

This exercise was so inherently satisfying—this elimination of words right down to the bones of my fascination—that I repeated the process over and over until the essence of the story had become poetry to me. The beautiful bones of a poem.

Then nothing happened. I checked out the book and brought it home. I tried to read about the other women's lives and found myself uninterested. I returned the book to the library and saved my few bones in a file. I applied for jobs as a professor. I went to Ukraine on a Fulbright. I returned to Colorado.

MEETING AGAIN

Years later, I attended a writing conference. Late one night at a picnic table under a New Mexican moon, I heard the words *St. Mary of Egypt*. Not once since I had written the words on my paper until this moment had I heard her name spoken by another person. I moved down to the other end of the table to listen. The speaker was a young woman who had recently converted to Orthodox Christianity and had chosen Mary of Egypt as her patron saint.

Listening to the woman talk, I felt conflicting feelings about Mary of Egypt rise to the surface. On the one hand, I suddenly recognized that I had long wanted to go out and join her in the desert. My own desire for solitude and silence could sometimes become the "unrestrained fervor"

that Mary spoke of so often. I wanted that kind of wild freedom—to
be completely hidden and alive in the heart of the desert. On the other
hand, I also wanted to invite her home. If shame kept Mary out there,
I wanted to wrap her thin, bare shoulders in a blanket; feed her more
than the few fingered lentils; and release her from every shred of self-
hatred that might keep her alone in the desert. The image of Mary of
Egypt, that night and many days and nights since, leads me again and
again to ask what I seek in the desert and what I want to bring home,
reconciled and healed but wild.

Mary's story—sensual and ascetic, holy and unholy, connected to God
but unconnected to all others, illiterate but deeply learned—seemed
to unearth my most basic longings, the ones that are etched so deeply
into my life that for fifteen years I have traced and retraced them with the
same paradox of knowing and not-knowing what drew me to that book
on the shelf in the first place. I am reminded of some lines from a poem
found in the Nag Hammadi papers from the first century:

> I am the whore and the holy one.
> I am the wife and the virgin . . .
> I am the barren one
>   and many are her sons . . .
> I am she whose wedding is great
>   and I have not taken a husband. . . .
> Why, you who hate me, do you love me,
>   and hate those who love me?
> You who deny me, confess me,
>   and you who confess me deny me.
> You who tell the truth about me, lie about me,
>   and you who have lied about me, tell the truth about me.

I began to make plans to explore the life of this Mary of the desert. I knew that exploration included the wild places of my own heart. I

wanted to ask what this holy one knows—in hopes that it would open new doorways and might lead to my own transformation in the desert wilderness, in my own complex interior.

My Old Life

But that was not all. By the time I went to follow Mary into the desert, the life I had lived for eighteen years was ending in ways that were outside of my control and far, far outside of my desires. The announcement of my old life's end came swiftly on a Wednesday morning in late August 2018, a few days before I was to leave for Cairo to begin my trek in the footsteps of Mary of Egypt. I had agreed to pick up Ali—one of my closest friends, who also happened to be my priest—at 5:30 a.m. and drive her over a mountain pass for a routine colonoscopy. The morning was bright and clear. I had not gotten up in time to finish my coffee, so I poured it into a travel mug and hoped the smell of it would not make her nauseous after she had been fasting all night.

Every week for nearly two decades, with few breaks, Ali and I had cooked and served a free community meal for fifty or more guests at St. George Episcopal Mission in Leadville, Colorado, sharing every aspect of the work. Our life together was mundane, made up of long walks, shared books, child raising, and how long to leave a turkey in the roaster at the church.

And poems. We spent the better part of these decades immersed in poems and ancient stories, as though we had unknowingly agreed to a long apprenticeship. In her sermons, Ali would often take a biblical text and point out how she had been arguing with it until its light had dawned on her and she had seen what was lying below the surface. She would follow this moment of grace with a poem by Rumi or Hafiz or Mary Oliver or Naomi Shihab Nye—her frequent favorites. I would leave these sessions savoring new language and new ideas in old stories as if they were flavors I had not fully tasted before.

That day I dropped her off at a hospital, but since parking on the narrow street in Vail was complicated, I drove on to a coffee shop to wait for her call. Later than I expected, my phone rang.

"Can you come?" she asked. Her voice sounded thin and shaky, like it had become sand.

But what kind of bad news was even possible? I asked myself as I drove out of the parking structure. This was a routine colonoscopy.

At the hospital, the doctor said that Ali had a mass in her colon.

"It's cancer," he said. Even though he was awaiting the official results of the biopsy, he nonetheless recommended she plan for surgery the following week.

The most significant crisis that Ali and I had ever faced came at an awkward moment. I was hours away from leaving on this trip that by now had been fifteen years in the making and two years in the planning. I would be away on a treasure hunt—that's how I thought of it—in search of an ancient wild woman. I intended to put my feet down in every place that was mentioned in the text that recorded her life.

"Maybe I should postpone," I said to Ali, "until your surgery is over."

"No way," she said. "I can't explain it. But I feel you are going for both of us."

CROSSING THE RIVER

Mary of Egypt was born along the Nile River in Egypt. As a young girl, she ran away from home. Maybe this occurred in the third century, maybe the fifth—no one knows, and there are no records. She ran to Alexandria, where she took up a life of spinning, begging, and most importantly, sex. She liked sex so much that she didn't even charge money for it, according to the document, even though she could have used the money.

One day when she was twenty-nine years old, she saw a boat of pilgrims headed for Jerusalem for the Feast of the True Cross. When she asked if she could join them, they asked if she had any money. When she said no, she offered her body to them in exchange for passage. The pilgrims took the deal. She arrived in Jerusalem several days later, still having sex with as many people as she could. She followed the pilgrims to the courtyard of the Church of the Holy Sepulchre, the traditional site of Jesus's burial.

In the courtyard, she tried to go into the church with the other pilgrims, but as she approached the door, she was mystically rejected. Every time she tried to enter, she was pushed back until she was left in the courtyard alone.

There she had an encounter with an icon of the Virgin Mary. In her encounter, she recognized that her spiritual condition prevented her from entering. She pledged to the icon of Mary that if she would be allowed to enter and see the True Cross, she would change her life. Whatever had been barring the door was lifted, and she was able to enter the church. When she returned to the courtyard, she asked the Virgin Mary what she should do next. From afar, she heard a voice that said, "Cross the Jordan, and you will find a beautiful rest." She took these words as instructions. She asked directions to the Jordan and was given three coins with which she bought three loaves of bread. She crossed over the river and lived for many years in the wilderness. In that wilderness, in the wild, she found freedom.

One day, the story says, forty-seven years later, a monk named Zosimas was crossing the desert. He was on his own spiritual quest, trying to free himself from the burden of extreme self-satisfaction. He saw Mary and thought she was a spiritual guru, one of the holy men of the desert, so he chased after her. When he found her and discovered she was a woman, he begged her to tell him her story. She did. Then she asked Zosimas to come again in a year and bring her communion. They met on the bank of the Jordan. Then she asked him to find her again in the wilderness in a year. The next year when he went to find her, she was dead. A lion licked the soles of her feet. Zosimas buried her in the desert with the lion's help.

* * *

This story had rung in me. I had recognized the ringing, but I didn't know what it meant. On the surface of things, I didn't have anything in common with this woman. I wasn't a prostitute, a runaway, or an abused child, and while I had some hermit-like tendencies, I wasn't a desert hermit either. Many Orthodox people I knew had an affinity for Mary of Egypt, but Orthodoxy had never drawn me in. Thanks to Ali, I was a reluctant Episcopalian with some Taoist inclinations.

Still, this had my name on it and would not let me go. After encountering Mary of Egypt that second time, my sketched-out notes from that day in the library were no longer enough. I began to research Mary's story in earnest. First, I turned to the scholarly texts. What do the scholars say about Mary of Egypt? How is she treated in the literature? But no matter how many books accumulated on my bibliography, reading wasn't what the story asked of me.

Maybe, I thought, *I haven't gotten close enough to the story itself.* Maybe the translation was getting in my way. One day at my desk at work in Chicago, I picked up the phone and called the library at DePaul University.

"If I wanted . . ." I said to the librarian, stumbling to articulate what I was searching for. "I mean, how would I find . . ." I was embarrassed not to have even the most basic knowledge of how to get a copy of the Greek text. But the librarian, with infinite patience, listened and pointed me to the *Patrologia Graeca*, a collection of writings from ancient Christians that included *Bios Mariae Aegyptiae*. He sent me a photocopy in the mail.

Holding the text in my hands was progress, but I didn't actually know how to read it. I stared at the squiggles on the page and rued the day that I had walked into Greek I at St. Olaf College and immediately walked out again. *Well,* I said to myself, *you have to start somewhere.* I called my dad, who is a Greek scholar.

"Dad, could you teach me Greek on Skype?" We began.

After two years of alphabet, conjugations, and declensions, I could pick my way through a text. We turned to Mary. With a Bauer's Lexicon, we started piecing together a translation of the *Life of Mary of Egypt* as told to St. Sophronius.

It was slow, messy work. Many lines of the text demanded not just an understanding of the words but an interpretation of Mary herself that despite all of my studying, I didn't feel prepared to give. For example, the text briefly describes the moment when Mary departs Upper Egypt for her life of prostitution in Alexandria. But the word that describes her leaving is ambiguous. It could mean that she "set aside" her affection for her family. This would suggest that despite her love for them, she faced something so traumatic that she ran. Or it could mean that she "rejected" their love for her, thus making her seem like a heartless adolescent who left despite having a loving family that did not want her to go.

Some of the questions also required us to make ethnic and even racial determinations that, again, I felt ill-equipped for. When the monk Zosimas describes seeing Mary for the first time, either he sees someone who has dark skin—"as if" they had been burnt by the sun—or he sees someone who after a long time in the desert has a skin color changed by the sun. One of these indicates an African saint; the other is more in the European and iconographic tradition of Mary that we have inherited. This might not have mattered a lot to the first readers of this text, but for me, it had implications I needed to acknowledge and explore.

When, at last, we had a translation, I did not feel like the itch was scratched. Translation had not given me a stronger understanding of Mary; it had provided a stronger understanding of the person to whom the writing of the story is attributed, a desert-dwelling patriarch named Sophronius. Translating this text, I didn't become Sophronius's biggest fan. He exaggerated Mary's "lust" at every turn for his own amusement. He lacked sensitivity to the realities a twelve-year-old girl might have faced in her society. He was far more obsessed with the parts of the story

I cared nothing about, dedicating chapters and chapters to Zosimas's education and decision-making as well as metaphors and references that did not feel relevant to my quest.

Sophronius's take on Mary of Egypt actually seemed to lead away from her and not toward her. She, the woman who had run away from Zosimas while he pursued her to the point of tears, was as elusive as ever.

Well, I thought, *that's because she is a legend, not an actual person.* She can't "speak through the text" because she is made of the text, not herself a maker. She is a myth. Nonetheless, I continued to accumulate files and footnotes. I tried occupying the mind of the only two characters in the myth: Mary and Zosimas, the monk. I read books about Jungian mythic structure and Christian myth making. I accumulated dead ends.

Here's the question I put to myself over and over again: Why? Why was I immersing myself in the life of Mary of Egypt? What was she offering me that I needed? Maybe my inability to answer this question was a character defect. Years before, when I had written my dissertation, my adviser would ask, "How are you going to answer the 'so what' question?" At home, I screamed into my pillow about the "so what" question. Later, when I worked as a journalist, a mentor asked me point-blank "So what?" when I proposed story ideas. Whenever she asked, I felt like a balloon leaking air. Then she would say, "It's a battle for the soul of America!"

"Right!" I would say.

But later, in my room alone, I would stare at the saggy little balloon of an idea and wonder how it could be a battle for the soul of America.

"So what?" I asked myself a million times.

As I studied Mary's context—the streets of Alexandria, the ports, Jerusalem, the vast Jordanian wilderness where she spent most of her life—I felt her recede ever more into the distance. She ran away from me as she ran from the monk, Zosimas, as if I stood on the edge of the same wadi, calling out, "Stop and give me your blessing." She did not turn around.

I felt out of options, but even with her elusiveness, I'd never encountered a saint more relevant to my own moment than this strange woman of the desert—rebel and repentant, lover and sinner, a hungry exile in search of freedom and rest. Her desire reverberated through the centuries as if she had spoken yesterday. Even though Mary had first come to me through a book on a library shelf, what she asked of me was not found in books. Where might it be found?

BEWILDERMENT

A question is a key, says Jungian psychologist and folklorist Clarissa Pinkola Estés. A question doesn't actually want an answer. It wants a door, a door into the psyche. In order to find this door, I could no longer treat Mary as a myth or as a text. She had to become a person, and the *Life* that I had so painstakingly translated had to become a map to find her. The key words became *as if:* as if Mary of Egypt had walked here, as if she had lived, as if she were a real human being.

This idea was exciting to me. Since I could not come closer to Mary in time, I would close the gap with space. I took the manuscript and mapped it out: Here are the places I needed to go. Here is the landscape I needed to walk.

Even while the idea grew on me, I recognized that it cut against my training as both an academic and a journalist. In neither of those disciplines is "as if" a legitimate category for exploration. "As if" was not solid ground. "As if" was like saying, "I have chosen naïveté over reason, myth over history." And yet I planned to take everything I had learned as a scholar and a journalist and apply it to my quest. I wasn't abandoning my trades, but I was using them in service of something further outside the realm of the ordinary.

Literary critic David Jasper makes clear his opinion that Mary of Egypt cannot be followed. "Mary of Egypt's silent life," he writes in *The Sacred Desert*, "teaches little or nothing, but in the act of reading it provokes puzzlement and a demand to be taken seriously. It has a harshness which claims no validity by any external standard and no possibility of reenactment—hers is not a life actually to be lived—but it makes its excessive demands in ways that are socially disruptive and destabilizing." So I interpreted this as, "Read about Mary all you want and let her mystery work on you, but don't go out there looking for her. She will not be found."

I became a pilgrim to the impossible anyway. The call of "as if" was stronger than the disciplining voices in my head. Of the archetypal Wild Woman, Estés writes, "In our bones, we know her, we yearn toward her; we know she belongs to us and we to her." *Go into the wild with Mary of Egypt*, I thought. Mary had lived her life by seeking larger and larger landscapes until there was nothing larger to be sought than eternity. I would seek the bigger sky to which she was called. Like Peter Matthiessen trekked after a snow leopard, I would trek toward Mary as toward an earthy but semimystical being. I intended to pass through another world in an attempt to meet her, even if I did not have an answer to the "so what" question.

Bewilderment, says the poet Fanny Howe, is a "way of entering the day" properly oriented. For her, bewilderment is a poetics, an ethics, and a theology all rolled into one. An Islamic prayer underscores this point: "God, increase my bewilderment." As I considered my state of bewilderment and the bewilderment into which my trip would take me, I found myself breaking the word into bits. "Be. Wilder. Ment." It felt like a directive. Be Wild. Be Wilder.

In the mythic world of Mary's story, no one ever makes spiritual progress by staying at home and thinking. To become a pilgrim is to take an inward journey by walking through actual time and space; one seeks the unknown world through both an inscape and a landscape. In other words, I had to go to the desert.

On long walks with Ali, I laid out this idea of walking Mary of Egypt's story "as if"—about turning a dream into a landscape and a landscape into a dream. Perhaps it was the long tutelage in scripture and poetry, but we both, without hesitation, felt a yes.

Unknown Egypt

I knew that I didn't want to show up in Egypt without a plan, but I also didn't want to sign up for a traditional tour, led along to look at mummies and pyramids, all the time wondering how to find Mary of Egypt. I didn't know where to begin. I did not speak Arabic, and I had never been to any of the countries where Mary of Egypt lived. Despite my obsession with the saint herself, I had never even been fascinated by this part of the world. It wasn't on my own personal bucket list. I'd never been drawn to pharaohs or sphinxes. I had no desire to see biblical sites or tombs. All I had was a scrap of a story, and that didn't seem like enough to build an itinerary.

But other things were falling in line: my grandmother left me a small inheritance. I checked in with Ali to see if she thought I could leave the Community Meal for a couple of months while I traveled and asked her if September and October would be OK.

Since this was before her diagnosis, she said, "Sure. Sounds like fun."

I asked my boss for some time as well, and he also agreed. Still, I didn't book tickets or find housing. I found myself paralyzed as I searched for some connection in Egypt that would signal to me that it was time to go.

One day, I wrote to Yehia El Decken, a member of a small company called Holiday Tours. For some reason, on this particular day, at this particular hour sitting in a hotel room in Chicago, I poured out my uncertainty:

Dear Mr. El Decken,

I am planning a trip to Egypt to research a late ancient Egyptian woman who is called, in the Christian tradition, Mary of Egypt. One strange part of this journey is that she may or may not have actually existed. But I am going to act as if she did and try to "follow in her footsteps," recognizing that this is a kind of postmodern quest.

The story goes that she was born and raised in rural Egypt. We don't know where precisely, and that is something I could use help thinking about. When she was twelve years old, she ran away from home and went to live in Alexandria. (This is approximately in the fifth century CE; some traditions say sixth, some say fourth.) In Alexandria, she lived as a prostitute, beggar, and spinner of flax.

When she was twenty-nine, she left Alexandria on a boat full of Libyan pilgrims who were headed to Jerusalem for the Feast of the Holy Cross. She basically sold sex to the pilgrims in exchange for passage. (From there, she had a mystical experience and ended up in the desert as a hermit.)

In my mind, the Egypt portion of my journey would involve the following:

1. *Some exploration of Alexandria, especially an understanding of its late ancient aspects. I am interested in how prostitutes lived. For example, I have read that the poorest lived "in doorways," but in my American mind, I can't quite figure out what this means. I have never been to this part of the world, so I am hoping for a more physical sense of all of this—not just things I am making up in my head.*

2. *I would like to travel along the Nile River to explore the Egyptian countryside. I would like to understand more about this way of life and the ecology of Egypt. Again, I have no idea what remnants of this time period are available to experience. But even to have a sense of the river itself seems important to me.*

3. *I have also been reading a lot about the Christian desert monasteries, and so I think I would like to have a more visceral experience of them.*

4. *And of course, I am interested in contemporary Egypt: people and food.*

I have heard that I should try to bring my husband or son with me in order to have male companionship. Is this necessary? I can bring one or both of them along, but this search is definitely mine, not theirs. They would come along to be nice. But if I need them, I need them, and I am sure we would have a good time. If you think that wise, I can work on this.

I am eager for your advice and would be grateful for whatever you can do. I recognize that this could be an odd challenge to take on, so if it is not right for you to help me, please feel free to pass this on to someone else.

All the best,

Amy

Not two days later, an email arrived:

Dear Amy,

Good day to you from Cairo. I received your email on Tuesday while driving, and my wife read it out loud, and I have to tell you that we both really enjoyed reading about Mary being a real person or maybe not. And we are interested to know about your findings and help your story.

The research is very specific. I like specific requests of people visiting my country because it's clear that they are appreciating our history and culture. I believe I can help you.

And no, you do not need male companions to travel in Egypt. But you might consider bringing some family. Egyptians are family people, and they will understand you better if you have your family with you.

I have to tell you, Amy, that your writing style is very nice.

Best regards,

Yehia El Decken

PART I
EGYPT

I keep secret in myself an Egypt
that doesn't exist.
Is that good or bad? I don't know.
—Rumi

Pilgrims abandon themselves to the breath of the greater life
that . . . leads beyond the farthest horizons to an aim which is
already present within, though yet hidden from sight.
—Lama Govinda, *The Way of the White Clouds*

BRING THE LIVE HEART

1.

While I sorted through my bag, deciding how much sunscreen and toothpaste to pack and whether I would need another pair of pants, Ali scheduled appointments and tried to figure out how to take medical leave from St. George. In the hours leading up to my departure, her news had gotten worse. The doctor had called to say that the biopsy had revealed "undifferentiated cells" that had not originated in the colon. This wasn't colon cancer, and there would be no surgery until they knew more.

She was clear about one thing: healing from this cancer, if healing was possible, required that she give everything she had for an indefinite period of time.

She met with an alternative medical practitioner in Boulder, a Russian woman named Larissa, who said to her, "Your surgery will pluck the flower of your cancer, and we will look for the root together!"

We were both headed off on elusive quests. Ali's quest had life-or-death consequences. She had to find the root of this cancer. For me, the stakes were admittedly lower: I was on a personal quest to find Mary of Egypt and to find out why she wanted me to follow her. We were both bewildered, and we were both on the verge of surrendering our ordinary lives.

At the airport, I texted Ali these lines from the poet Rumi:

And if you bring a dead heart carried like a coffin on your shoulders, God will say, "Oh, cheat! Is this a graveyard? Bring the live heart! Bring the live heart!"

The first leg of my trip was from Denver to Detroit. I had arrived at the airport in plenty of time—time enough to think about Rumi and text Ali. But as the flight boarded, a young gate agent called me to the desk.

"Your passport, please," she said, and then typed away at her computer entering the information.

"And your visa?" she asked.

"My visa?"

"For Egypt."

"I don't need one," I said with breezy confidence. "I can get one at the airport in Cairo for $25."

"I'm sorry. You must have an e-visa confirmation. You were supposed to have brought a copy with you to the airport."

How had I missed this crucial information? I felt panic rising.

"Why did you think you didn't need one?" the woman asked. "Where did you get that information?"

I hesitated. I knew how silly I would sound.

"My mother told me."

Never had that answer sounded so shabby. Since Yehia had suggested that I bring family, I had asked my mother to join me on the Egypt leg of the journey. I had turned over to her a lot of the logistics for the trip because she was good at logistics—much better than I was. I wanted to explain to the woman behind the desk that my mother was an accountant, a detail person. I took her word for it because her word was good.

You don't know my mother, I wanted to plead. Instead, I waited for the gate agent to respond.

The agent jotted down two websites on a luggage tag where I could possibly get an e-visa at the last minute. I took my computer over to the side and started entering information. The websites to which she had sent me repeatedly spewed out an ominous answer: "The visa must be issued at least seven days in advance of departure."

I went back to the desk, thinking frantically. My mother planned to meet me in Paris, and she was already on an airplane. I couldn't call her for help. Maybe they would let me go as far as Paris. Then I could sort it out with her. Or we could even hijack the whole adventure and hang out in Paris for a few weeks. Why not?

"No," the agent said. "Without a visa, we can't even let you on the plane."

The plane had completely boarded. The gate area emptied. Three agents were now gathered around the computer screen that said I needed to have an e-visa. They had begun to talk rapidly in agent-speak, exchanging authoritative acronyms.

At last one of them said, "This one says, 'No visa required.'"

"But the other one says, 'E-visa required.'"

They stood in silence for a moment. The trip hung in the balance at so early a moment, I had to wonder if I had subconsciously sabotaged it.

"Well." They all looked at me. "Let's go with this one." They shrugged a collective, bureaucratic shrug. The young agent handed me my boarding documents. She smiled. I boarded.

I hoped my mother hadn't been wrong about this. From the beginning, she had managed our hotel bookings and kept track of tickets. She was a bold traveler, but this journey was ad hoc by design. Even with Yehia's help, we were mostly winging it. Mary of Egypt's path wasn't well marked by tourist hotels and air-conditioned buses. I crossed my fingers and hoped that she was truly up for what we had started to call The Quest.

2.

In Paris, my mother and I sat together in the waiting area for our plane to Cairo. Across from me, I saw a woman with a streak of gray in her dyed red hair. She drank a Coke Zero as she scanned her iPad, her feet propped up on her roller bag.

American, I thought. "I wonder if she has a visa," I said out loud.

"We don't need visas until we get to Cairo. We'll get them in the airport for $25," my mom insisted with authority. She was dressed in a long white tunic and leggings. We had discussed at length what to wear in a conservative Muslim country. This had been her solution. Mine was a pair of Patagonia linen pants and a light long-sleeved shirt.

But it was clear when we arrived in Cairo that whatever we were wearing, there would be no hiding our foreignness. A woman dressed in a full burka, only her eyes showing above her veil, took us under her wing in the passport control line. Her eyes were intensely expressive as she guided us with small gestures, making sure no one stepped in front of us or misused our uncertainty. I felt a burning desire to ask her why she had decided to attend to us, where she was coming from, where she was going. But the passport control line was not the place to interview her. She underscored for me all that was unknown about this trip. Eyes and hands. No more.

My mother was right, of course.

We bought our visas in the airport for $25 each.

As we walked out into the hot Egyptian night, we saw a crowd of Egyptians gathered to meet travelers—among them, a young man with a sign that read "Mrs. Amy Frykholm" in clear black letters. In a pink polo shirt and khakis, he looked like a prep school student. I reached out instinctively to shake his hand, but the light return grip surprised me. I wondered if I had done something wrong.

Mohamed, the young man, spoke excellent English. He helped us load our bags into a white van and told us about his studies and his work for

Yehia. We told him about The Quest, and his eyes lit up in what would prove to be only our first misunderstanding. What happened next would happen again and again in Egypt.

"Oh yes! Mary of Egypt. Actually, my uncle did a radio show about her!"

"Really?"

"He did, yes! He even traveled like you are describing to Jerusalem and followed in her footsteps."

"He did?"

This was amazing. A lead on the first day in the first hour to someone who had already done what I was going to do? Maybe Mary of Egypt was more well known here than I expected. Maybe this would be easy after all. Maybe this was a miracle, a sign. Or it was too good to be true.

"I would love to meet him," I said.

"I will see about it," Mohamed replied.

Later that evening, I finally met Yehia—the tour guide whose letter had proven to me that even on the other side of the world, my quest might be understood. He was younger than me by some ten years and had as live a heart as I could have hoped. We sat at a Coffee Bean and Tea Leaf on the Nile island of Zamalek in Cairo. He told me that Mohamed had been anxious about picking us up because he might have to shake our hands. In Mohamed's practice of Islam, people of the opposite sex don't touch if they aren't related. I thought back to the light handshake and cringed at having made such a mistake.

"But still," Yehia said, "he likes you, and he wants to help you with your work. He told me he thinks you are interesting people. He thinks most women your age in Egypt are sitting around eating *mashi*."

"What's *mashi*?"

"Stuffed vegetables."

FIND THE ROOT

1.

"Do you want to see some pyramids?"

Yehia and Mohamed were in the front seat of Yehia's Skoda Octavia, and my mom and I were in the back. We were on our way to an overnight train to Aswan, the first stop on our Mary of Egypt origins tour, and everything had gone better than we had planned, so we had some time to kill.

I wasn't big on seeing pyramids. Before I left for Egypt, numerous people had asked me, "Are you going to see pyramids?"

"It's not that kind of trip," I said. The pyramids had been built at least three thousand years before Mary of Egypt's time. I was sure they were interesting, but I had different plans.

But if Yehia thought we had time to glance at some pyramids, I wasn't against it. We drove along Cairo's traffic-stuffed streets. Horns honked constantly. Cars and motorcycles wove through traffic, with everyone looking for any open space. From my angle, it looked like an incredible exercise in intuition. Drivers had to make calculated guesses about the moves of people around them and follow slight signals. Later I learned that there were whole vocabularies of gestures and honks that drivers were using to make this work. For this woman from the wide-open dirt roads of South Dakota, the enterprise was astonishing.

"Pyramids!" Yehia called after we had been driving awhile. We looked up at enormous gray rock a few steps from modern apartment buildings and shops—massive reminders of a time utterly other than the one we were in. "I often think," Yehia said, "that the pyramids must have been made with love; otherwise they never could have lasted so long."

I had always equated the pyramids with slave labor—naked men hauling rocks a great distance under duress. The introduction of love puzzled me.

"I don't have any proof," he said. "I think they must have been made this way because things that are not made with love and respect are never well done. This is not true of the pyramids. They have lasted this long and will continue."

As we turned back toward the train station, past shawarma cafés and cell phone stores, Yehia opened up a Wi-Fi hot spot on his phone.

"Metastasized ovarian cancer," Ali wrote via text. Stage three. Surgery had been delayed. Treatment options being considered. "I feel like I am looking for Mary too," she added. "Your desert friend."

2.

Mohamed waited with us at the train station. Our train was late. We watched trains pulling in, packed with people throwing themselves at open doors and hanging off the trains' ledges.

"Where are those trains going?" I asked him.

"Aswan."

"How long are they going to hang on like that?"

"Maybe twelve hours. Don't worry," he said, shrugging. "Your train won't be like that."

We were headed "up" the Nile, south toward the Egyptian region of Nubia, on the border between Egypt and Sudan. Yehia had recommended this as a starting place for our search because traditional ways of life were still in evidence. There were islands in the Nile where people lived as they had for thousands of years, without cars or electricity. They herded sheep and made traditional crafts. If I wanted to see what Mary's birthplace and early life might have been like, Yehia thought Nubia would be a good place to start.

As the train chugged through the Egyptian countryside, I noticed the very thing I had read about in so many books: the sharp demarcation of the landscape. The Nile valley was lush with green fields, palm and banana trees, donkeys carrying sheaves of wheat, and people working the fields in long robes. Behind it were sand-colored hills rising at the level of the horizon without a hint of green. Life, not-life—the contrast was stark. That made the choice that the early desert hermits had made even more startling. They had gone into those barren hills to demonstrate that the place that everyone thought of as a place of death was one of eternal life.

Nubia had been a separate kingdom for much of Egypt's history. Modern Egypt had incorporated Nubia in order to dam the Nile and create a more stable agricultural environment for the rest of Egypt, the result of which had not been great for Nubia. Thousands of Nubians had been displaced when the dam was built. Many had died in the desert, and many more had never returned home.

When Christianity was introduced to the region, it resisted. After the region became Christian, it then long resisted Islam but now was almost entirely Muslim. In many ways, the civilization hinted more toward Sudan than Cairo and toward the headwaters of the Nile, thirty-five hundred miles to the south in Ethiopia—sharing food, architecture, and other cultural markers with these neighbors.

The *Life of Mary of Egypt* notes that Mary's skin was dark: "The one he saw was black in body as if burned by the sun and had hair that was as white as if it were wool, and this hair was short not even reaching the neck."

In the iconography of Mary of Egypt, developed over centuries and largely in Europe, her hair is often long and her skin pale. The text described her differently, and as we went farther south in Egypt, people's skin darkened. It reminded me that the woman I was looking for came from the continent of Africa. She had been Europeanized by a tradition that Europeanized all of its saints and major figures. But she was, in fact, African.

As I looked out at the domed houses and the donkeys, at the Nile and the desert, I remembered my question about the relationship between myth and history—about whether it mattered if Mary had walked the earth with real feet or if she had merely been the figment of some desert monks' imaginations. The landscape told me that that I was in the territory between the two, and the demarcation was not as sharp as that between desert and river valley.

3.

The train arrived late in Aswan, the capital city of Nubia. Even though we had brought some snacks with us, we were still starving when we got off the train. We hoped the guide meeting us would say something about lunch, but instead, Mido said, "Yehia called me and said to take very special care of you, Dr. Amy and Mama Meeshel."

He whisked us around to the main sites of Aswan: the Unfinished Obelisk and the Isle of Philae. Mido loved monuments. Mido, I could tell, loved monuments more than food or rest. My mother and I clambered over slick granite under a sun that was hot and getting hotter, sweating and hungry.

"You are not interested in monuments." Mido's face fell when I suggested that we needed food and shade.

In the folder that he carried, I had seen an index card on which he had written English phrases he wanted to use to help us understand the place we were in, to learn its history. He had written "triumph over enemies" and "wage war." Something about these phrases, this index card, and Mido's careful preparation to meet two off-season American tourists endeared him to me.

"We might just need to eat something first," I said. "And then we can see more."

Yehia had arranged for us to stay in a Nubian village west of Aswan where the streets were sand and camels had the right of way. In a domed guesthouse, a man named Goma served us a cold ginger drink. We walked along sand streets to a restaurant where dish after dish of curry and delicious Nubian bread were served to us.

We talked about Egyptian politics, the fate of Nubia, and Mido's love life.

Mido's full name was Abu Bakr Hussein Said. Mido, he said, was his mother's flourish, but the name suited him. It set him apart: sophistication mixed with tenderness. Nubian was his first language, Arabic his second, and English his third.

"I want to get married," Mido said. "I am looking. But I want a woman who . . . I want to travel . . . I don't like routine, everything today just as it was yesterday. I want. . . . But she must be smiling, cheerful. That's the most important thing."

My mom gave me a doubting look. I could hear her thinking, *With this kind of reasoning, Mido will never get married.*

The next morning, I woke up in a place that felt like a dream: the sand streets, the random camel, in front of me the wide Nile with ibis and heron drinking from it. A bright woodpecker made its presence known in a cassia tree. Pink-and-white bougainvillea cascaded over the shore and fence lines.

I got up early to watch the sunrise. I was up too early. A woman still wrapping her braids in a scarf looked startled to see me appear on the street. The village dogs weren't too fond of me, shooting me confused looks as though asking why I couldn't behave properly, like other tourists. I felt like an intruder on the intimacy of a village accustomed to having a little time to itself in the morning before being observed by tourists. Or a pilgrim posing as a tourist.

When I tried to take one path, one of the dogs sat on my feet, while two others started barking. When I went the other way, a group of children found me and began practicing their English.

"Good morning," they said.

"Good morning."

"What your name?"

"Amy."

"Amy."

"Phone?"

"Do I have a phone?"

"Phone?"

"No."

"Money?"

"No."

The Nubian islands of Seheyl and Hessa were—to my sight—granite-covered hills with adobelike houses built amid them. Seheyl was flatter with more sheep grazing. Hessa was topsy-turvy, a jumble of steep climbs and boulders. When Mido showed us the plots of land he had bought to perhaps create some kind of ecotourism business, I struggled to see anything but rocks. *Maybe*, I thought, *this is why Mido loves monuments: they are rocks transformed into meaning, rocks you can learn to read.*

Yehia had wanted me to see the stability and sustenance of this way of life, almost untouched by modernity. I observed that people worked in the morning, slept in the heat of the afternoon, and walked around at night. They kept things simple: no manufactured objects except those made by their own hands. They were not in a hurry and did not seem to long for what modern conveniences could offer. The river gave the life that was needed.

But I also noticed that while hospitable, the people didn't live in a public way. On both the island of Seheyl and the island of Hessa, we were invited into the outer courtyards of people's lives—a liminal space between public and private. There we were met by people who had been designated ahead of time to meet tourists, and we interacted with them in a culturally prescribed way. On the island of Hessa, a woman named Mona greeted us in the outer room of her home, where we were urged to lie down and rest on beds that had been set up for this purpose. For us, this was strange. We weren't accustomed to lying down in a stranger's home. But it was a simple signal that public and private, inside and outside, were organized differently here.

Later in her life, Mary did not have access to the private life of a home. Once she left Egypt, home was not something she ever knew again. Instead of inner rooms, she lived in doorways. Instead of family spaces, she made a home in the wilderness. "A rock gave her shelter," the Orthodox version of Mary's story says. Being in Mona's house with its cozy connections between various family units, an intimate courtyard, and places for hospitality made real that loss.

Historian David Frankfurter writes about the significance of boundaries and thresholds in late ancient Egypt. The house served as a complex of protective boundaries against supernatural penetration that could bring ill effects on an entire family. One Coptic manual specifies the supernatural protections that should be applied to the entrances and exits, windows and courtyard, bedrooms, open rooms, foundations, and so on—anywhere people crossed over thresholds from one space to the next. These were perceived as vulnerable spaces in need of special protection. When Christianity began to compete with more ancient rituals and belief systems, individual households created their own combinations of protective religious symbols to integrate the new religion into the old.

The most important threshold for late ancient Nubians and Egyptians was that of the river itself. Every spring, the river overflowed its banks in an event called the inundation. This flooding determined how large or small that year's harvest would be. Because of how central this was in the lives of the people, the religious rites and traditions that Mary of Egypt would have observed as a child centered on the Nile. Even generations after Christianity came to Egypt, people greeted the river's inundation with rites and incantations that had been a part of their lives for at least a millennium. Religions—early Egyptian, Christianity, and later Islam—did not displace the river as the center of spiritual and physical life.

4.

My mother and I were finding it easy to get lost in the magic of Nubia and Mido's love for it. Clues for Mary of Egypt were few and far between; word from Ali was scarce. Sometimes I felt like Odysseus, who ends up on the Isle of Ogygia with Calypso for seven years, forgetting his quest completely. We could float around on boats with Mido forever, sipping ginger drinks, and it wouldn't be long before we asked, "Mary who?" It seemed awfully early in The Quest to lose track of it completely.

One evening Mido took us up to the rooftop of his house, which looked west and south over the Nile. His sister, Aya, had spread a carpet for us on the roof and then arrived carrying a table on top of her head. She put the table down and smiled. Her light-green abaya blew in the wind as she arranged cushions for us on the ground.

The sun began to set and turned the river gold and silver. Aya reappeared with platters of fish and rice and flatbread. As we ate, the sky darkened, and stars began to appear.

For a moment, Mido disappeared, returning with coffee-making supplies. He turned the table on its side as a windbreak and built a fire. He toasted green coffee beans in a long-handled spoon over the fire, added cardamom, and then ground the coffee. With ginger and clove, he added the coffee to water he had set on the fire to boil.

"I don't really drink coffee in the evenings," my mother said, trying to be helpful amid Mido's dramatic flourishes.

"Shh, Mom, jeez," I muttered, embarrassed. "This is the coolest thing that's happened so far in Egypt."

Mido used dried palm as a small broom to filter the coffee and then poured it into tiny china cups. He sipped and frowned. "Too much ginger," he said. "Oh well, tomorrow you will have real Nubian coffee."

Mido and I sipped our coffee and lay out on our cushions to look at the stars, stretching out under the Egyptian sky as if it were home.

5.

Where in the world are you? I love saying that. Yesterday I moved from panic to numbness, probably because I was in mama-mode, telling the girls. In Chinese medicine, "cancer" is called fire toxins. I may choose those words—fire toxins—over "cancer."

Larissa has asked me how strong I feel in my desire to face this. She then looked at my face and said, "You don't have to answer. I can see from your face that you are determined. OK."

Where in the world was I? Under Egyptian stars while Ali made appointments and tried to make sense of her health insurance, call doctors, plan a surgery. Throughout my adulthood, Ali had been my North Star. She had been there at the birth of my son. She had baptized him with a big seashell of water and then let him pour the water on her in turn. She had read poems to me and breathed new life into the religion of my childhood. She had cooked the Community Meal and believed with me in its imperfect hospitality. In her I had found someone to whom I could tell my dreams, someone who could hold them lightly and turn them over in her hands without clinging. She was my priest, my confessor, my friend. The doctors were telling her that she had a 25 percent chance to live three years. Losing her would mean losing what I knew my life to be.

And what of Mary of Egypt? Was she somewhere under these stars, along these sand streets? Was the root of her here? The Nubia through which I walked in search of her continued to feel like a kind of dream. One morning a little girl jumped out at me after breakfast, braids flying. She shook key chains at me, saying, "One dollar. One dollar." The key chains were figures of Nubian women dressed in traditional clothing. I dug some coins out of my bag and gave them to the girl. I looked for Mary, figured in a key chain, and I thought, *No, she is not here.* Later, a guide pointed to the ceiling of an ancient monastery where faded frescoes could still be seen. "There she is," he said. "Mary of Egypt." I looked closely. It was a woman, yes. A forgotten Christian saint, another footnote. But not my Mary.

My Mary had left long before that fresco was painted, and she didn't leave much of herself behind. She had slipped out in the night, maybe, or had been stolen away, kidnapped, or sold. No one knows. But she had not left a mark on her homeland that I could find, wherever it might have been. That had been as she intended. She had left without a trace.

From here, she had traveled to Alexandria, the big city. Then to places now named Israel, Palestine, and Jordan. Her story was written into *The Golden Legend* and carried to England and France and Germany. There was a time when she had been the most popular saint in Europe. She herself had walked relentlessly onward, out from whatever home was offered to her, erasing her footprints behind her wherever she went.

Even though Mary had left Nubia, I didn't think Nubia would easily leave me. *Noureso.* It was the only Nubian word I learned. "You are light to me." In the *Life of Mary of Egypt*, there comes a moment when Mary expresses her longing, ever so briefly, for the Egypt she had left behind. Now I knew a little of what that meant, and I could hold a little of that inside me.

On the train out of Nubia, I received another text from Ali. She wrote that she was headed to Florida to an alternative treatment center. Her surgery wouldn't be scheduled for a month, and she couldn't imagine sitting around feeling the cancer growing inside her and doing nothing.

I can't believe I just put a deposit down for an insane amount of money spent on three weeks to try something. I feel so soft, absorbed, and lost. I know that you, my friend, are somewhere very far away looking for something you are not sure is real. Right now, I don't feel real because nothing that I used to identify with makes any sense.

6.

When a Wild Woman comes into being, is she running to something or fleeing from something? Who tells her that the rules and the structures of society may not have her highest good in mind? Who sets her out on the way, shows her the path?

When Mary begins the narration of her life to the monk Zosimas, she begins with the simple statement, "I myself, brother, had Egypt as my homeland." Then she adds, "When my parents were living and I reached the age of twelve, I set aside my affection for my family and went to Alexandria."

These few lines collect a multitude of mysteries, and legends of Mary throughout the ages have tried to fill in the blanks. Did Mary reject a loving, close-knit family? Or did she flee a violent one?

In the Middle Ages, when versions of Mary's life proliferated across Europe, poets created a kind of Princess Mary from these lines. She was a beautiful woman who came from a noble family, and she ran away from privilege and affection because of selfishness and foolishness.

Glorified and fairy tale–like as this version is, it had never made much sense to me. Family position and patronage weren't just nice perks in late ancient Egypt. They were life itself, especially for women. To run away was to cut yourself off from the sources of life and of meaning. To become family-less was to choose destitution and hopelessness. Even at twelve, you would only do this if the circumstances were dire, if you were certain that in staying where you were, things could only get worse.

As the train chugged back to Cairo, I tried to imagine what it would have been like for Mary to flee. What specifically did she escape when she left—a violent father, an unwanted spouse, poverty? Had she been sold to strangers or kidnapped by them? Did she travel on foot or by boat or by donkey cart? Had her journey been arranged or did she improvise? Was she beholden, as so many trafficked people are today, to the people who helped her travel? Or was she so alone she could only hope that no one would see her? Did she travel the distance of six hundred miles by herself or in a caravan? Was she helped by the kindness of strangers or trapped by circumstances she did not understand? Any way it went, the journey had to have been undertaken in fear. Maybe she also had a modicum of hope that she was running *to* something as well as away from something, but that was impossible to know from my distance.

I looked out at the fields where grain was gathered and dried, where the people cultivated melons, tomatoes, and cucumbers. This was the world through which she ran from the only life she had ever known, following the river downstream toward the sea.

CLIMB TO THE HIGH PLACE

1.

In response to my desire for a "visceral" understanding of the relationship between Christian monasteries and the story of Mary of Egypt, Yehia had arranged for us to visit the Monastery of St. Anthony, the oldest Christian monastery in the world. While Mary had certainly never been to this place, and it was far from the sites of her life's action, Sophronius had chosen to base his *Life of Mary* on a story about the founder of this monastery. It was a tale that would have been well known to his audience, and he wanted his readers to connect that narrative to Mary of Egypt. I wanted to understand why.

The story goes like this: During the time that Anthony lived in a cave, before he founded the monastery, he had a dream. He dreamed of a man whose thirst for holiness was even greater than his own. Anthony was urged to "go and seek this better monk." Guided by prayer and mystical experiences, he left his cave to search, and he found the monk, Paul of

Thebes. Paul had lived alone in the desert for decades, and he was old and near death when Anthony found him.

Today there are two monasteries, St. Anthony's and St. Paul's, that sit thirty-five miles apart from each other, separated by desolate hills. Monks traditionally undertake hikes between the two monasteries. But Yehia told me that he himself has set out several times to find the route between the two monasteries, wanting to be guided by dreams, mystical experiences, and prayer like Anthony was, and he has not found the way. Each time he has tried, he has turned back.

"Why don't you just ask the monks?" I said.

He smiled a little sheepishly. "I want to find my own way."

On the surface of things, Mary's and Anthony's stories have little in common. He was the first Christian monk; she was a prostitute. They lived in different landscapes, probably in different centuries. But in Mary's story, Zosimas, the monk, is like Anthony: Zosimas goes in search of more—more holiness, a deeper connection with God, a companion, a mentor, a guide. Mary is like Paul: she is the one hidden in the deeper desert, whose holiness surpasses anything that Zosimas has previously imagined. In both tales, the good monk learns the better monk's name, hears their requests, receives gifts, and deepens their understanding of spiritual life.

But the two accounts are different. Paul, for example, has a less dramatic backstory. He fled to the desert as a young man after the death of his parents and lived in a cave for more than a hundred years, as the legend has it. None of the resonances of sex and repentance are present in Anthony and Paul's story. The stories are different enough that before our visit, I couldn't see what point Sophronius might be making.

The day we set out to visit the monastery was the Lunar New Year, a holiday in Egypt, and the roads out of Cairo were clear of traffic. The night before, I had mistakenly wished Yehia a "Happy Muslim New Year." He corrected me. It was the *lunar* new year. The moon, he said, belongs to everybody.

Mohamed—the young man who met us at the airport on our first night—agreed to accompany us. He had never been to the monastery and wanted to see it. I knew he had mixed feelings about going to such a Christian place, and I hoped my mother and I could be sensitive enough to that to make him glad he had come.

After we headed out from the city, with its crumbling nineteenth-century villas and its green belt of river, the landscape quickly became desert. It wasn't desert like I knew from Utah and Arizona, covered in cacti and sage, scrub brush and piñon. This was a more barren desert than I had ever imagined: bare brown hills, one after another. After an hour or so, the Red Sea appeared on the horizon as a glimmer without warning. Then a mountain materialized the same way—through the haze, gradually taking shape.

A note had arrived from Ali. She was in Florida at the alternative treatment center. "It's hard," she wrote, "to find myself in my body right now. Where is my home ground? The Florida heat bakes and grounds me. Are you finding the essence of Mary? Clues?"

The immensity of what we were facing with Ali's cancer stared back at me like the desert. I had been saying to my mother and to myself that it felt "unreal" that Ali had cancer and that, for her, everything was changing, including her relationship to Leadville, to St. George, to me. But as I watched the empty brown hills shape themselves into mountains toward the sea, I thought that what I meant by *unreal* was that it was too big to feel. If I started to feel what it might mean to lose Ali, what my own life would be if she were not in it daily, I would feel an abyss. If someone said to me "You have to start feeling it," I would hear that as an impossibility on par with "Walk across this desert." I wouldn't know where to begin, and I wouldn't trust that beginning was a good idea at all.

After driving for a while along the Red Sea, with its hulking, now empty resorts, we turned sharply to the west, where the desert loomed again. Gradually, in the distance, we saw two hills, and those two hills became the Monastery of St. Anthony. When we pulled into the gates,

I thought we might be the only visitors, since we had driven so far out into the desert and had seen no other cars. I was startled. I had often heard the refrain "The desert becomes a city." Scholars use it when they talk about the rapid growth of Christian monasticism around the time of Anthony. But I didn't expect to see an actual city, with tour buses and children playing soccer in the wide expanse of the parking lot. There was a small market, hotels, restrooms, and a canteen, surrounded by a wall.

Within the wall was another sand-formed wall. Inside of that containment was the monastery. We walked inside and were immediately greeted by a monk who called himself Father Lucas. He was a tall, thin man in his thirties. When we asked him where he came from, he smiled a gap-toothed smile.

"When monks come here, they forget where they came from. They take a new name. Everything from before is forgotten. So"—he laughed— "I forgot!" But he had been trained as a dentist before he came to the monastery, he said, and he still worked several days a week in a free clinic the monastery runs for locals.

Father Lucas was one of the only Egyptians I met who had heard of Mary of Egypt, and when I mentioned her name, he said, "The Russians love her!" Later I understood that while the Russian Orthodox liturgy contained a version of the story of Mary of Egypt recited every year during Lent, Coptic Christians used an earlier liturgy that did not contain Mary's story. This is one of the reasons I found so few traces of Mary of Egypt in Egypt itself. She had not been remembered in liturgy here.

Mohamed and I were already figuring out that the Mary his uncle had followed for his radio show was Mary the Mother of God, not my more humble and less well known Mary of Egypt. This confusion followed me on my pilgrimage and was buried deep in the name itself. Miryam, Miriam, Mary, Maria—this name of the Universal Mother in all three major Abrahamic religions. I had wondered if Mary of Egypt called herself "Mary" in order to erase all that had come before. Perhaps she meant, "I don't need a name, but if you need one, take that of my spiritual guide, Mary the Mother of God."

After Zosimas had met the strange woman in the desert and heard her story, he became desperate to know her name and frustrated that he had forgotten to ask. When he returned to her one final time, she was dead, and he despaired that he would never know it. But he mysteriously found words written in the sand near her body: "Bury, Father Zosimas, at this place, the remains of the humble Mary. Render dust to dust, and always pray for me to the Holy One."

When she finally gave him her name, she gave the Name Universal, as if she, like Father Lucas, was saying, "I forgot!" At the same time, she claimed one of great significance in the Christian tradition, a name that crosses boundaries and reveals as much as it hides.

2.

Father Lucas guided us through the monastery beginning with a place called the Chapel of the Four Creatures. St. Anthony believed that the four creatures of Revelation—the human, the lion, the ox, and the eagle—were expressive of the life of a monk. You enter the monastery as a human being, he said, with a human being's limitations and contradictions. You become a lion as your intention grows fierce and the work difficult. Then you become an ox, a laborer, putting one foot in front of the other in the name of simple holiness. Finally, as you work, you are transformed into an eagle.

Father Lucas gave us a few minutes to take in the atmosphere of this tiny interior room. The silence was so thick, it had texture, the accumulation of seventeen hundred years of continuous prayer. I wanted to sink down, lean against one of the brightly painted walls, and become silence myself.

But we pressed on to walk among the monastery's many frescoes. Father Lucas pointed to one saint's gesture: one fingertip touching another fingertip.

"It is the sign of eternal life," he said. "Here there is no death," he continued. "Only translation."

As the tour continued and he showed us images of the many monks who had died, I wondered what he meant. I thought of a line from Goethe: "Die and Become. Until you have learned this, you are but a dull guest on this dark planet." I thought of Ali, at this moment across the world, grappling with the reality of her own death. Cancer could—probably would—kill her.

Become. Translate. What did Father Lucas mean?

Mohamed and I decided to climb the 1,158 steps to Anthony's original cave. Father Lucas smiled a little at our decision, made at midday.

"It's lovely in the early morning," he said. "And I've enjoyed it in the evening. In the middle of the night, it is quite nice to climb up there. But in the middle of the day? I can't recommend that." He arranged for my mother to settle in the guesthouse with tea and dates and then guided us to the place where the stairs began.

Mohamed and I started the climb. The sun burned our heads. Our legs burned too. Not one step was easy.

"You know that sura in the Qur'an?" I said to Mohamed. "The one that says 'Allah intends ease for you and not hardship'? I don't think there is a verse like that in any Christian Scripture. I think in Christianity, you are supposed to suffer."

He laughed. We kept climbing. I thought about St. Anthony's Four Creatures. You start the climb as a human, with a little bit of ambition and no small amount of false pride. But if you are going to continue, you have to turn into a lion, fierce in your intention. And eventually, if you go far enough, you are just an ox, putting one leg in front of the other for no reason you can remember. And maybe, eventually, you can become an eagle. At least that's what I longed for at about Stair 700.

"Why don't you teach me how to count in Arabic?" I said to Mohamed. "Maybe the climbing will go faster."

"*Wahed*," he said.

"*Wahed.*"

Ethnein. Talatha. Arba-a. Khamsa.

We repeated the numbers over and over again. Each repetition brought us closer to the top until in front of us was the cave. We hadn't been flying exactly, but somehow it did feel like the last five hundred steps had been more effortless than the first five hundred. I forgot the climb itself almost immediately as I looked into the narrow opening of the cave.

We left our shoes and backpacks by the opening and went in through a slight passage with towers of gray rock on either side. Through a small opening, near an altar, a young caretaker for the place, a local boy hired by the monks, was reading on his phone. Every time he swiped, the phone made a small swooping sound that punctuated the silence.

As we sat down, sweat started to pour off my body, until I thought that if I sat still long enough, I might become a pool of water. The idea of melting in the cave of St. Anthony was comforting. Give up The Quest, stay still and quiet forever. Evaporate.

"I don't know," Mohamed would say to my mother. "One minute she was there, and the next she was gone. Translated."

For Mary, disappearance hadn't been a fantasy. She had disappeared from her family; she disappeared from Egypt; eventually, she disappeared into the wilderness. Maybe, following in her footsteps, I could disappear too. Maybe that's why she couldn't be followed. Everyone who tried disappeared.

I thought again about the story of Anthony and Paul that Sophronius had used as a model for his story about Mary and Zosimas. What had Sophronius been after when he had taken the story of two holy men and transposed it into an encounter between a holy monk and a former prostitute? The discovery of Paul was not a surprise to Anthony—once he'd had the dream, he knew what he was looking for. But Mary's holiness was a surprise to Zosimas, a sign of God's radical grace. She had become so refined spiritually that she could walk on water, she could hear conversations that took place miles away, she could levitate. She knew, through a strong gift of God, all about Zosimas's own life.

Mary disrupted Zosimas's assumptions. He didn't find Paul, as he expected. He found Mary, in whom human expectations were overturned by the God of love, the God who "does not detest anyone." To the pious monks of his own day, Sophronius's message was, "You want to see what holiness looks like? It doesn't look anything like you." While the story of Paul and Anthony might lead a monk to say, "I've got to try harder," Mary's story might lead a monk to say, "I am not sure I know what holiness is." Sophronius confused the categories.

Back out into the sunshine, something had loosened in Mohamed. He slid down the banisters and then ventured out on the rocks, looking for an alternative way down. He joked that if my mother had climbed all of these stairs, we would never get down, because as an inveterate picker-upper of trash, she would have had to save all of the water bottles people had cast over the edge of the stairs.

The cave of St. Anthony had set something free in him, and I didn't know what it was. The look of perpetual anxiety disappeared from his face.

The trail down from the cave had had a levity, an ease, but now the drive back to Cairo was long. We each slipped away into our own thoughts. On Mohamed's Wi-Fi hot spot, I heard from Ali:

I've learned that I don't breathe very much. I think of Mary Oliver's poem, "Are you breathing just a little and calling it a life?" I have been practicing a quick inhale. I have found I am too familiar with the sad sigh, that long exhale. But the sound of surprise, delight, astonishment—I am not as familiar.

I know intuitively that there could be some benefit in being able to think past this diagnosis, to imagine being alive past it. What comes to mind is that I would dream of taking the beginner's QiGong class. I would love to learn to do it and offer it to others. It would be a way to be a wounded healer. But that kind of hope is actually very, very painful because I am not sure that is going to be available to me. I resist hope because it is too scary.

As I write this, a strange little animal just walked up to me. It looks like an anteater. He was wandering around until he noticed me and then backed up, surprised, and ran away.

I wrote back,

I can't think of any animal that looks like an anteater but isn't.

Then I watched the setting sun spread bright red across the desert, and tears started to roll down my face. I was melting again.

SIFT THROUGH
THE SAND

1.

From her homeland, wherever that had been along the Nile, Mary arrived in Alexandria, the metropolis of her moment. Today the city is a chaotic mix of ancient and modern: donkey carts piled high with electronics, pillars and tombs amid high-rises and crowded streets. While the modern world looked like it had won whatever battle had transpired, the slightest glance down at our feet reminded us that the whole operation was built on sand. Left to its own devices, I thought, Alexandria would disintegrate. Impermanence was its hallmark.

This made the problem of searching for Mary of Egypt here evident. Everything in this city eventually became sand or sank into the sea. The entire ancient imperial port of Alexandria was now being excavated one marble pillar at a time from the bottom of the Mediterranean. My non-professional opinion was that there had simply been too much marble for the shaky ground to bear. Nevertheless, a French excavation team was doing their best to retrieve it.

I knew that Alexandria had been home to one of the greatest Christian schools of thought, the school that produced the theologians Clement and Origen, still influential today. But no one knew where that school might have been located. You couldn't visit. The fact that it had once existed was of little use to me as I stared out across the high-rises toward the sea. The great Library of Alexandria that had once housed perhaps as many as four hundred thousand scrolls had been completely destroyed by 250 CE, before Mary's time, but had been in decline for hundreds of years before that. It had been replaced by a modern building, completed in 2002, which was beautiful and inspiring, but it couldn't give me a sense of what Alexandria had been.

We had wanted to be in Egypt with the intent of pilgrims, not tourists. We didn't want to glance at things the way a tourist might. Egyptian Museum. Check. Pyramids. Check. Trip along the Nile. Check. In some of the literature on early Christian pilgrimage, scholars had made a distinction between *glancing* and *beholding*. Beholding was the pilgrim's work. To me, beholding meant a way of looking that called for a more fine-tuned and patient attention. In beholding, there might be contemplation and wonder. Curiosity, yes, but not of an insistent kind—the kind that is open to experience and open to the heart's whisperings.

It wasn't entirely clear what to behold in Alexandria. And pilgrims, as I understood it, typically followed established routes and were given things to contemplate, sites to visit, milestones to observe. We did not have this established route for Mary of Egypt. I had pieced together our itinerary drawing from bits of information, geographic clues, and Yehia's advice.

We had to create the experience of the pilgrim in a place where time had been insistently at work erasing what was left.

Our one hope was a place called Kom el-Dikka (Pile of Rubble). Kom el-Dikka had been discovered in 1967, when ground was being broken for a new apartment building. The apartment building had never been built, and a Polish archaeology team had started an excavation. The grounds were expansive, with baths, a Roman villa, an amphitheater, and a variety of ruins representing rooms and workshops. The layers of multiple eras were revealed—the crude construction of later times built over the more precise Roman stones.

Alexandria was established on the Mediterranean eight hundred years before Mary's time, and for more than fourteen hundred years, it had been the capital. When Mary arrived in Alexandria, she would have seen a city, once a jewel, now in decline. "Alexandria," I had read in the guidebook, "once home to the wonders of the world, continued to fall from grace as each new ruler built less memorable structures and layered over the ancient city."

Maybe to Mary it was a beacon, but the civilization that had given it its form had started to crumble and add its rubble to the sand. In Mary's time, Alexandria would have had a mix of people, languages, dress, and manners. Greeks, Copts, Syrians, Romans, North Africans, Europeans—any of the peoples who traveled the Mediterranean might have stopped in the port. For Mary, the sea might have represented a place that opened up to the entire world. Maybe that is why she chose the sea as her way out when the time came to leave.

Given my question about beholding and glancing, the only thing I knew to do at Kom el-Dikka was to find a place out of the sun and sit. Among the ruins, I tried to imagine the life of a person who was said to "live in doorways."

We know that Mary's role in these layers was involvement in the sex trade. In Alexandria at that time, if you were a woman and sex was your business, you would have three choices. The first was that you could become the courtesan of a wealthy man. Of these options, this one had a semiofficial aspect. It had a modicum of respectability and comfort, even status, associated with it. A courtesan had some of the benefits of the patronage system, and this was the most secure form of nonmarriage available to a woman. As a courtesan, you had food, shelter, a social setting, and a livelihood. But we know that Mary of Egypt was not a courtesan.

The second was that you could become an actress. Women who performed onstage were considered sexually available by the mores of the day, and they might be required to perform sex acts with other actors or with people who attended performances. Alexandria was famous for its theaters, and Kom el-Dikka had been a center for performances. It had the only amphitheater in Egypt. But there is no sign that Mary of Egypt performed onstage. That leaves us with the third possibility and the one that makes the most sense: the street trade.

My mother and I sat in a part of the complex that was at a remove from both the amphitheater and the baths where there was a series of small rooms that would have been reached from a staircase that descended from the street. These rooms could have been workshops or small stores. They could have been rooms attached to an inn. Here you could imagine Mary attracting customers at the street level and bringing them down into a place like this, where a room was little more than a doorway.

Street prostitution was considered the lowest form of prostitution and the most dangerous. Street prostitutes were often the property of pimps, who might even have brought them to Alexandria and now required them to work to pay back their travel expenses. They had little form of protection in a society that required it. If Mary was a prostitute here, she would have wandered in this place, where squalor pushed up against former grandeur and people did what they could to survive.

I pictured Mary in these rocks, making a home out of no home.

2.

But the *Life of Mary* offers a different view of Mary's role in the street trade. When Mary tells Zosimas about these early days in Alexandria, she mentions no pimp, no gangster or pirate, no abusive father or violent spouse. She mentions nothing about the trafficking of women. Here's how Mary tells Zosimas of her own life in Alexandria: "When my parents were living and I reached the age of twelve, I set aside my affection for my family, and went to Alexandria. Right from the beginning, I destroyed my virginity and without self-control I threw myself into the passion of sexual intercourse. I am ashamed to think of it."

Months before I went to Alexandria, I told this first part of the story of Mary of Egypt to my sister-in-law, Kelli, and her sister while we were working on putting insulation tape around the windows on the back side of Kelli's cabin.

"She ran away from home," I said, "and went to the big city of Alexandria."

"Why did she run away from home?" Kelli asked. An obvious and important question.

"The text says that she left because she loved having sex so much, she had to get to the city, where she could have as much sex as possible."

"Right," Kelli said, shaking her head while she stood on the ladder with the tape in her hand. I held out a pair of scissors to her. Her sister held the ladder. "That sounds like a man saying something he wants to believe about female motivation."

"Of a twelve-year-old?" her sister added. "That's just creepy."

As I sat at Kom el-Dikka, looking at those little rooms, I saw something that even in my translating and mulling and itinerary planning, I hadn't seen. The text doesn't actually say that Mary went to Alexandria *because* of sex. It only says that as soon as she arrived, she started having sex. All the whys are blank.

Mary was a runaway. Maybe she felt the allure of the big city. Urban life was considered far superior to rural life. Maybe she'd overheard people talking about the great, beautiful Alexandria—the theaters, the markets, the baths—and she wanted to see for herself. Mary would become famous forever because of her wanting, her thirst for more life than was presently available to her. Maybe that longing overtook her, even at so young an age.

But there are bleaker possibilities. Sale. Abuse. Sex is still often the means used to run. Sell what you have and get where you need to go or away from what you need to flee.

In Mary's case, we don't know how she ended up in the sex trade. She herself assigns no villains. When she tells the story, she puts the responsibility of choice in her own hands. She erases any and all others who might have culpability. Or maybe Sophronius records the story in such a way that only the women are to blame.

Mary insists to Zosimas that she had sex because she *liked* it, and she wanted to have as much as possible:

> But now, I will say this thing briefly, for it seems noble that you may know the state of my passion and my love of pleasure. For seventeen years, forgive me Father, I continued to devote myself publicly as a fuel for debauchery. And it was not in order to receive payment from others, I swear, for many times they wished to pay me. Instead, I intended to do this thing in order to achieve my own satisfaction. Do not, however, suppose that I was well-off, and for that reason did not accept money. I begged to support myself and often I spun flax, so that I could devote myself to insatiable and unchecked lust, to roll in that mud. This to me was life: to make of myself entirely an insult to nature.

"Don't you dare imagine me as a victim," I hear her saying. "I was the instigator. I was the perpetrator." We can dismiss that agency and imagine Mary as the victim of a corrupt and abusive system devoted to the exploitation of young girls. Or we can say that she just liked sex. But neither of these options help us much to grapple with the complexity.

Some historians have wanted to give Mary exactly the agency she demands. Historian Virginia Burrus, who offers a wonderful burlesque reading of Mary's story, says Mary "enjoys sex too much to reduce it to an economic transaction." Patricia Cox Miller adds to this, emphasizing the same freedom that Mary gives herself in the text. Mary, she says, is "not attached to a *leno*, a pimp, or indeed to any man, unlike most prostitutes who had little control over their bodies and were subject to legal regulation." Both scholars read Mary as a "sex radical" who commands her own pleasure and takes her own path.

Sometimes I think Sophronius (or Mary via Zosimas via Sophronius) is making a kind of grim-humored joke: "Of course, I didn't take money. Someone else did. Some guy named Antoniou or Beshotep or Tausiris. Me, I did it for the pleasure."

3.

Nightfall is hard. And that is when I just want to be held. Hot, familiar skin is the only thing that works when I have my nighttime breakouts. I have glimmers of hope yet fear those glimmers as well because they are so vulnerable.

I am feeling afraid to be in my body but finding it difficult to get any sense of groundedness without it. My body is where the cancer is. My body is where this secret was kept from me. How do I go there?

I am eating tons of garlic and turmeric. I smell strange when I sweat. Who is this person?!

But yesterday I had an amazing breath work session with a QiGong person who is seventy years old—tiny, strong accent, black skin, white hair. I don't know where he is from. He directed me to breathe in certain ways, and a lot of intense emotion came out. I was sweating and exhausted afterward yet buzzing like I was filled with electricity.

Ali had been anorexic as a young woman. Over the years that I had known her, she had gone through different phases of understanding anorexia in her life and her recovery from it. She knew that buried inside of her was a desire not to show up for life's demands. Anorexia was a form—a powerful and deadly form—of not showing up, but there were other ways to fail to show up for life. "There are many ways to starve yourself," Ali told me.

Anorexia is, among other things, a disorder of desire. You take a natural thing like your body's own hunger, its impulse to eat, and then you twist it around into a tangle.

Ali had taught me to be respectful of desire. Yes, she said, the religious tradition that we are a part of often disparages desire and calls it dangerous. But desire is a path, a door, a leading. If you pay close attention to your desires and are respectful of them, you are on a path toward wholeness, which can also be translated as holiness.

Both she and I responded to our culture's disordered approach to desire by feeding people. The church was open almost seven days a week with food. We served five free community meals and hosted a large food bank. There was almost never a time that you couldn't walk into the church and get fed. My son, as he grew up, became almost instinctively hungry the minute he walked into the church. No sooner had we passed through the red door and into the entryway than he would say, "Mom, I'm hungry." Then we would go on a hunt for snacks.

Ali and I knew that both hunger and its satisfaction are every bit as theological as they are biological. The connection between the communion table and the community meal is only one of degree. The communion table is a more symbolic form and the community meals a more embodied form, but their intimate relation is undeniable.

Because of Ali's teaching, I was inclined not to dismiss Mary's expression of "insatiable desire" as either a male fantasy or an emblem of religious oppression. The Christian tradition, of course, has a lot of ways to talk about sexual desire, most of which are cautionary tales with troubling outcomes. For example, lust is a sin among the seven claimed to be most deadly. Mary of Egypt is traditionally interpreted as someone consumed by it. What is lust? One view is that lust is the use of another person to gratify one's own desire. It can't lead to love because it is blocked inside itself and its own need. And lust, at its most extreme, fails to acknowledge the humanity of another person. It is what Martin Buber might call an "I-It" relation. The "It" is the "object" of your lust. Lust in this sense is a diseased pathway. It cannot lead to love.

But another view of lust is that it may contain a seed of true longing—the longing for the other. Without this longing for something other than the self, there is no life. Longing—and therefore even lust—can be a pathway to love.

4.

My mother and I walked down to the place in Alexandria where the people's port would have been in Mary's day. Where the water met the shore, the heat shimmered. Young entrepreneurs had set up chairs and umbrellas along a strip of sand, and they charged a small fee for sitting. At midday, the chairs were empty. We were the only takers.

We looked out at dinghies and fishing boats, some of them with reed-covered roofs and frayed fabrics blowing in the breeze. Others had reed baskets piled on top of cloth-covered roofs. Amid buckets and baskets and nets, the shore had an ageless, ramshackle appearance. It could have been the nineteenth century or the sixteenth. If you squinted, you might see the fifth.

This was the place where Mary might have first spotted the boats and the pilgrims that so filled her with desire that she felt she had to leave Alexandria. The text says, "One summer day, I saw Libyan and Egyptian men in a large crowd running to the sea. I asked the person next to me, 'Where are they running to, these men?' He answered, 'They are all going up to Jerusalem for the Exaltation of the Honored Cross, which will take place in a few days, as usual.'"

I tried to imagine the scene: a crowded seashore where fishermen mixed with marketeers mixed with newly arrived and newly departing merchants, slaves, and sailors. In the chaos, the pilgrims themselves might have been easy to miss. But Mary depended on ever new clientele. She probably saw them immediately. What she might have seen was people hungry for adventure and on the move. She saw opportunity and she took it:

I said to him, "Will they take me with them, if I want to go?" He said to me, "If you have the ticket price and the money for your expenses, no one will prevent you." But I said to him, "Truly, brother, I have not acquired money either for the ticket price or for the passage, but even so, I am going to go with them. I am going to go up into one of those boats they have hired, and they will take care of me, even if they don't want to, for I have this body that they will receive instead of passage."

Just as she predicted, the pilgrims accepted sex in exchange for passage.

On pilgrimages, people from various classes and genders flowed together, sleeping in the same cemeteries or on the docks of the same ships. Social distinctions were undermined by movement. The unpredictability of the road helped create possibilities, and this meant that the rules shifted. Travel created desire. Desire undermined the accepted order of things.

Church authorities were not always thrilled about pilgrimage for this reason. Jerome, an early church father, was notoriously grumpy about it. Even though he was in Bethlehem and people came from all over the world on pilgrimage to see him, he still asserted that you didn't have to come to Jerusalem to experience a holy life: "By the cross I mean not the wood, but the Passion. That cross is in Britain, in India, in the whole world. . . . Happy is he who carries in his own heart the cross, the resurrection, the place of the Nativity of Christ and of his Ascension." And Gregory of Nyssa, another early patriarch, astutely noted that people have a hard time walking with holiness through landscapes where "passions lurk."

The pilgrims that Mary encountered did not seem particularly interested in the contemplative aspects of pilgrimage. They were young men with a spirit of adventure, on the road to see something new. They were counterevidence to historian E. D. Hunt's assertion that "the pilgrim on the road saw himself as engaged in an enterprise of pious devotion." Mary's pilgrims were more like people taking advantage of the means their culture made available to answer that innate human hunger for the road.

As Mary continues her narration of the journey, she certainly describes the ship as more pleasure cruise than pious undertaking:

> How to narrate the things that happened then, O man? What kind of tongue could declare or ear possibly receive the things that occurred in that boat during the journey? The things that I forced on those unwilling young men? There is no kind of licentiousness, spoken or unspoken, which I did not teach those miserable ones. I am amazed, my Father, how the sea bore up under my debaucheries. How the earth did not open its mouth and lead me alive into Hades, I who trapped so many souls. But it seems that God was seeking my repentance. For God does not will the death of the sinner, but remains patient, waiting for the turning-around.

In this account, Mary would have us believe—once again—that she alone is responsible for what happened on that boat. It was her "shamelessness" that drew the pilgrims. She "forced" sex on these "unwilling young men." It's a description that might be laughable, yet I don't get the feeling we are supposed to laugh.

Even if I don't laugh, I find I want to celebrate the freedom Mary sought using what means she had. She was bold, brave, adventurous, and resourceful. She sought that bigger sky, the more of life, running from forces that would contain her. And on the other hand, she was a woman traveling alone without protection, without patronage. She would be a target for rape, for violence. Women alone in that social world, as Mary tells us she had been from the age of twelve, would have been the most vulnerable, the least respected, the least defended.

How do we understand the dual nature of Mary as the perpetrator, as she so clearly insisted to Zosimas, and Mary as the victim of a system dead set against her, a system that she tried to use to her advantage but could not always have been successful? I am left with this double lens when I think about Mary, the boat, and her agency.

What I do see, however, is the way that Mary's desire drew her outward, just as desire had drawn me from the comforts of home in an attempt to find her and myself. When the Wild Woman is on the move, we are disrupted. Estés writes, "She whispers from night dreams, she leaves behind on the terrain of a woman's soul a coarse hair and muddy footprints. . . . She is the voice that says, 'This way, this way.'"

Now having sipped hibiscus juice in Nubia, watched the sun set from Mido's roof, watched camels dominate the streets, talked philosophy with Yehia, and sat on the floor of St. Anthony's cave, I was no longer satisfied with the question, Was Mary a victim or a perpetrator? I knew the pull of the foreign and the unfamiliar, the way travel could fill you with desire, could expand your heart. *Maybe*, I thought, *Mary is an icon of desire*. We know the Wild Woman takes the world into her own hands. Estés describes her as "the knife of insight, the flame of the passionate life, the breath to speak about what one knows, the courage to stand what one sees without looking away, the fragrance of the wild soul."

Unlike Mary, I didn't want to leave Egypt. Egypt had given me a sense of aliveness I couldn't remember having experienced in years. Look, look what the world is full of! Look how beautiful it is.

Ali texted me, "When Mary was leaving Egypt, what do you think she was feeling?"

"Desire," I replied.

Before we left Egypt, my mother and I sat again along the coastline, this time close to where imperial Alexandria lay at the bottom of the sea. It was a windy day, and we watched big waves break on the rocks. Families sat near the water; a few people swam, but the surf was rough. A young man was trying to take a family out for an excursion on a little rowboat, but he couldn't get through the breaking waves. He kept trying to move out into open water but was sent back again and again into the bay. Meanwhile, a man made tea on a coal fire that he built on an old stone Ottoman wall. The wind blew from the west. It might have been good weather to sail to Jerusalem, but no boats were going that way.

Part II
ISRAEL

Therefore, I will now allure her,
   and bring her into the wilderness,
   and speak tenderly to her.
From there I will give her vineyards,
   and make the Valley of Achor a door of hope.
There she shall respond as in the days of her youth,
   as at the time when she came out of the land of Egypt.

—Hosea 2:14–15

BE ASTONISHED

1.

In Mary's day, it was easier to travel from Alexandria to Jerusalem than from Alexandria to the Monastery of St. Anthony. Mary's route by boat was a frequently traveled one. Depending on wind speed and direction, it could be a journey of only a few days. The pilgrimage routes were routine, marked with inns and hostels. Even if Mary had landed on the Mediterranean coast of Israel with no idea where to go, she still could have followed the masses to the nearest hostel and then gone with the crowd on the road to Jerusalem.

My mother and I would gladly have gone by boat, leaving right from the coast of Alexandria and sailing to the coast of Israel, docking at the ancient port of Jaffa. Instead, to travel the five hundred miles from Cairo to Tel Aviv, we left Cairo in the evening to fly nine hundred miles east to Jordan and then back west to Israel. There is no easier way. You cannot fly directly from Egypt to Israel, even though the two countries border each other. Travel between them is largely restricted.

We didn't arrive in Tel Aviv until long after midnight. We had booked a hotel on the internet months before, and we gave the address to the taxi driver, an elderly man who told us emphatically of his love for Tracy Chapman as we listened to her sing "Give me one reason to stay here" along the streets of Tel Aviv.

When we pulled up to the address we had given the driver, we all stared at the sidewalk in confusion. There was nothing there that looked like a hotel, and the neighborhood looked like a warehouse district.

"Are you sure this is it?" the driver asked us. We shrugged and mumbled something about the internet.

He got out of the car and stood for a few moments on the sidewalk and then walked around the side of the building. I hoped he would get back into the car and say, "Let me take you to a nice place that I know."

Instead, he opened the trunk and set our bags on the sidewalk. "OK. It is here. Around the corner."

Inside the brightly lit lobby, a young man with a long ponytail stood behind a desk arguing with a woman in a combination of English and Hebrew. Another woman sat silently on a chair nearby with a Bluetooth headphone in one ear. She appeared to be tuning out the argument, which was about her. Would she be allowed to spend the night in the hotel without a passport? This appeared to be the question the other two were discussing.

The desk clerk interrupted his argument to hand us a key to our room. When we reached it, we found a tiny, hot cubicle with loud music pounding through a thin plywood door. I looked at my mother with a small amount of desperation. She looked back at me with the same. Where were we? I turned on the air conditioner. It immediately turned itself off.

I carried our bags back down to the desk. "We are leaving," I said to the young man. "Please give us a refund."

"No, no, no." Another man, small with the pointed features of a bird of prey, had joined him at the desk. "We have a quiet room for you. Just a moment."

As we waited, I saw the two women outside smoking at a café table set up on the sidewalk. They were not speaking and appeared to be waiting for something or someone. I could not tell how the argument had been resolved. The two women drew my attention. I felt something sinister that I couldn't name, not about them, but about the world they inhabited, a world that we now bordered.

The room the second man took us to smelled of boiled cabbage, but at least the air conditioner functioned and the room was relatively cool and quiet.

"This will . . . work," my mother said.

We fell into a thick sleep. I dreamed of sandy streets and a small, slight man in a gray robe who looked like Goma, who had served us ginger drinks in Nubia, or like the man Ali had described, Bodie, as I imagined him. He kept appearing and disappearing along the street as if leading me somewhere. He had crumbly bread with him, just like the street crumbled and the edges of the dream crumbled.

I woke up thinking about the two women downstairs: trafficking. This is how Mary of Egypt arrives in Israel.

2.

As I had studied maps and planned the trip from the distance of the United States, I pondered trying to walk from Tel Aviv to Jerusalem, as Mary would have walked from Jaffa to Jerusalem. A scholar showed me a website where you can pretend you are in the ancient Roman Empire and type in where you want to go and how you want to travel. It will then show you the routes. The website was fun to play with, but it didn't reveal in any practical terms how to attempt this.

Instead, we called a cab. Our cab driver's name was Avi. As we loaded our bags, he said, "If I may ask, how did you end up in this hotel? It is a hotel for . . . for . . . immigrants, for . . . Africans."

My mother and I looked at each other and wondered if we could laugh now.

"The internet," my mother said.

But as we drove out of Tel Aviv toward Jerusalem, I saw graffiti on a post. "Africans back to Africa," it said in English.

Maybe this was also how Mary of Egypt arrived in Israel—already rejected, already outcast, having to make her own way any way she could.

Avi dropped us off at the place where we planned to locate ourselves for the Israel part of The Quest—the Tantur Ecumenical Institute, on the boundary between Jerusalem and Bethlehem and walking distance to the heart of both cities. For the first time in our travels, we were pilgrims amid other pilgrims. We settled into a dorm-style room; made a quick tour of the grounds, with a library, chapel, and dining room; and took some deep breaths. We poured ourselves cups of coffee and tried to get our bearings.

Jerusalem was a city of holy places—so we and millions of people before us had understood. People come to Jerusalem from all over the world to see holy sites of Judaism, Christianity, and Islam, and they have been doing this for many centuries. Holy places are those marked by a story of divine intervention, where the divine has touched the boundary between the material and the spiritual. When a human being brings her own physicality to this site, she also partakes in some way of the holiness. The spiritual power of it perhaps becomes available in a new way.

This kind of pilgrimage was different than the earlier "beholding" that my mother and I had been doing. We had been bringing a kind of attention to the ordinary—to doorways and pathways, to particular arrangements of rocks. No one, to my knowledge, thinks of Kom el-Dikka as a holy place. It's a historic site where one can learn and explore a way of life that is different from one's own. But the particular finger of the divine is not there as it is said to be in Jerusalem, rich with holy places that invite you to think about who walked where and how the place came to be set apart.

This kind of travel has now become inexorably intertwined with the language of advertising: "Walk in the Footsteps of Jesus." "Our 9-day tour of the Holy Land will transform the Bible into a vivid reality." "Prepare yourself for a life-changing journey to walk where Jesus walked." Buy now. Sign up now. This product offers instant transformation.

That sense of the commercial also pervaded our experience as pilgrims.

While faith by travel in Mary's day was not quite as successfully advertised, it shared an underlying belief that by seeing and doing—by being in the presence of the holy places—you could be changed. The fifth century, when Christian pilgrimage really got going, was not an otherworldly moment in the history of Christianity, historian Peter Brown says. People were exploring the connection between faith and geography. As they saw, heard, smelled, and felt the places where Jesus walked or Elijah was fed by ravens or John was baptizing in the Jordan, they also wanted some small material object to remember the place by. They filled tiny flasks with holy water or pocketed pebbles from holy sites. All of this made the holy tangible, the ineffable concrete.

Modern pilgrims are still turning the holy into tangible reminders, bringing inner and outer lives together through objects and sensory experiences. This was, indeed, in at least some senses, the purpose of The Quest. I had thought that maybe if I put my actual feet on the ground close to Mary's well-hidden tracks, I might understand something I didn't understand before. I might know why she had called out to me through the fissures in my life.

But this was not Mary's purpose when she arrived in Jerusalem. She was not interested in making the holy tangible. She was interested in the tangible itself—new sites to explore, new smells, new sounds, new languages, and perhaps most importantly, new bodies to touch. Mary was after novelty. She made her way into the city "satisfying herself" with "many others . . . citizens and foreigners alike," whom she "picked up for ·this purpose."

That made being a pilgrim in search of Mary an incongruent experience. Our plan was to do what pilgrims to Jerusalem normally do: as my mom put it, "Go see the holy stuff." But we were holding that in tension with the fact that our Mary didn't—at this moment in her journey, anyway—care much for it.

3.

Following the smells of baking bread, sage, and rosewater, we made our way through the Damascus Gate and into the Old City of Jerusalem. Like Mary, we followed pilgrims. There were Russian pilgrims in spiky heels and Sri Lankan pilgrims in saris. There were Spanish pilgrims following behind large wooden crosses that had been rented for the day and American pilgrims in shorts and tank tops. We planned, on our first day, to find our way to the Church of the Holy Sepulchre, where Mary had her life-changing encounter with Mary the Mother of God.

Not only were most other pilgrims headed in that direction, but we learned after some practice that no matter whom you asked for directions and where you were asking to go, the local people of the Old City took one look at you and pointed you in the direction of the church.

The Church of the Holy Sepulchre was built on the site where Jesus was said to have been crucified and resurrected. It has been on this site since the early fourth century, when the empress Helena, the mother of Constantine, traveled to Jerusalem in search of the holiest of Christian sites. She was pointed by local people to this place, and she claimed it and had a church built on it. The church, as it exists today, is not by any means the original. It has been burned to the ground more than once over seventeen centuries. Wars, famine, earthquakes, and plagues have all had their way with the site, and yet it remains the nexus of Christianity.

As a pilgrim of Mary of Egypt, I was perhaps most interested by the part of the church that most pilgrims hardly noticed: the courtyard. In the story of Mary, the courtyard is where she had her life-changing encounter with an icon of Mary the Mother of God. I wondered if an image of Mary the Mother of God would still be in the courtyard as it had been hundreds of years before. I also wondered if there would be any sign of Mary of Egypt's famous pilgrimage. With so many stories and so many centuries piled on top of her, what would remain? Did people still come to see the remnant of the True Cross, as the pilgrims in Mary's day had? I had timed my trip to Israel to coincide with the Festival of the True Cross because of Mary's itinerary, but I didn't see any sign of that festival.

The place was thick with people anyway, as it would have been in Mary's day. We sat for a while on the stone steps outside, watching the scene. Pilgrims in matching T-shirts and pilgrims in matching brightly colored tunics. Guides with baseball caps held up on poles. Pilgrims with devices in their ears to hear their guides better. Everyone, everyone taking selfies. People flowed in and out of the wide front doors, sometimes pausing to kiss the doorposts or cross themselves on the threshold.

There was no image of Mary the Mother of God in the courtyard. There were no images of any kind. After taking in the scene, we followed the crowd into the interior. It wasn't a church like any other I had been in. It lacked a central focal point but was built as a series of passages without anything that resembled signage to help people find their way. It felt more like a dreamscape than a church, one of those dreams where you walk and walk—down and up—looking for something that never appears.

Disoriented, we followed the crowds and did all the things we saw pilgrims and tourists alike do. We climbed the stairs and stood in front of the gaudy chapel marking the crucifixion; we stood in line outside a little nineteenth-century chapel called the Edicule, which was built over the rock where Jesus's resurrection was said to have taken place; we watched our fellow pilgrims bow and pray and even weep.

I left feeling a deep sense of disconnection. We had been at the holiest of holies—at a place where our religion, the religion we had practiced all of our lives, had begun—and I left feeling like we'd been in a labyrinthine museum. We'd stared at things, watched our fellow pilgrims like they were from another planet, and then dragged ourselves home on a bus wondering what it was for. I imagined that if Ali had been with us, she might have sparked my imagination, given me some piece of poetry that might have interpreted it for me.

4.

I had not heard from Ali in a few days. I tried to picture her in Florida among anteaters. She was finishing her time of treatment and preparing to leave for a consultation at Dana Farber Cancer Center in Boston. She had written that one day, in the midst of a treatment with Bodie, she felt something move under the covers of the treatment table. "Bodie!" she called out. "I think there's something there!" It was a small salamander in the sheets.

After our lost feeling at the Church of the Holy Sepulchre, I did what I suppose my academic instincts told me to do: I went online to see if I could understand the church better and perhaps school myself in how to see it. As I scrolled through websites, reading descriptions, I was startled to find a reference to a chapel in the church dedicated to Mary of Egypt. No book I had read over my years of research had mentioned it. The website said, "As one faces the main entrance, to the right is a disused stairway that was the Crusaders' entrance to Calvary. At the top of the stairs is the Chapel of the Franks. Beneath it is the Greek Orthodox Chapel of St. Mary of Egypt—a prostitute who was converted in the church courtyard in the fourth century and spent the rest of her life as a hermit."

Didn't I feel like an idiot? All of these years spent planning this trip, and I hadn't even managed to learn of the Chapel of Mary of Egypt, right there in plain sight—right in the courtyard where I had watched people come and go. For all my desire to behold, I was an ordinary tourist after all, stumbling around staring at things with no idea what I was looking at.

The next day, my mother and I went back to the Church of the Holy Sepulchre, determined to find the chapel. This time, every other person in the church seemed to be Russian. Russians crowded in the courtyard, followed priests around, kissed icons, took selfies. *Maybe it is a special Russian day at the church*, I thought.

I stared at the front doors. There was the staircase and the Chapel of the Franks. Beneath it was a small, inconspicuous metal door. I went up to it. It was locked. To the right of that was another little door. It too was locked. I went inside the church. There was no chapel opening from the inside either. Maybe the internet was just wrong.

I found a Russian priest and asked him. Even though I had studied Russian in college, I couldn't come up with "Mary of Egypt" in Russian on the spot. Was it *Svyataya Mariya Yegiptskaya*? Or *Mariya iz Yegipeta*? And what was the right word for *chapel*?

This is it, I thought. *You spend years studying, you travel halfway around the world on a quest, and you get stuck on a language quiz you didn't know you were taking.*

It turned out that the young priest understood English better than I could speak Russian. "It is outside and to the left," he said clearly. "But it is closed."

"Closed?" I repeated. "Closed for how long?"

His face hardened in a way I couldn't understand. "It is closed," he said again.

We went outside and stared at the front door again. Then we tried all the doors along that side of the church's courtyard until a man in a white shirt and sandals who sat on the steps stopped us.

"Here private," he said.

"I am looking for the Chapel of Mary of Egypt," I said. I tried in Arabic, "*Miryam al Masreya*."

He gestured to an open door on the other side of the courtyard. *Maybe he is just trying to get rid of us*, I thought. His gesture was so matter-of-fact, so practiced, as if twenty people a day asked about the Chapel of Mary of Egypt. That alone made me suspicious that we were not going the right way.

As we stepped across the threshold of the chapel to which he had pointed, coolness and calm washed over us. This place was set apart from the madness and heat of the sepulchre. There was an atrium and then a small worship space with an iconostasis and pews. I kept my eyes peeled for signs of Mary of Egypt—an icon, an image—but I saw nothing.

In a narrow alcove, we saw an icon of Mary the Mother of God.

"This is a very famous icon," the caretaker, who had followed us into the alcove, said. It had split open many years ago: a crack appeared in Mary's left eye, and then water began to flow through the crack, as if she were crying. Thousands and thousands of people used to come to pray with this icon and to see the miracle.

We sat for a few minutes in the coolness of the chapel, looking at the cracked image of Mary. Every time I asked about Mary of Egypt, someone led me to the Virgin Mary. It felt like Mary of Egypt was teasing me.

"Why are you looking for me? Here's the Queen of Heaven. I am pretty sure she's the one you wanted to see," I could imagine my Mary saying. To Zosimas, she had been quite blunt: "Why do you seek, Father Zosimas, to gaze upon a sinful woman? What do you so long to hear or to see from me that you are willing to undergo such a labor?" She could have said the same to me, but instead, she kept pointing me to images of her spiritual guide.

Later we walked back out to the street with vendors calling to us, "Sit and have coffee with me, madam!"

My mother said, "You know, when I get home, people are going to ask me about my pilgrimage."

I felt a pang of anxiety. "What are you going to tell them?"

Dead ends, closed chapels, and a lot of images of Mary the Mother of God?

"I guess I am going to tell them about The Quest."

She said this lightly, with no resentment, as if the process drew her and she was not attached to its outcome—as if The Quest were a real thing.

5.

But The Quest was not a thing; it was a verb. *Questing*, we should have called it. When you look back on a treasure hunt, it is easy to forget the dead ends, the wrong ways, the missed guesses. The next morning I woke up thinking, *Is this the way? Maybe we are doing this wrong. Maybe we are seeing the wrong things, doing the wrong things. Maybe this isn't a pilgrimage after all. Maybe we should just become tourists and see all the stuff we are supposed to see.*

Somehow I felt like I had been talking to Mido in my sleep. I had been asking him, "Tell me about your faith. What is its bedrock?" I had been talking to him about seeing all the rocks out of which my religion had been made: the rock where Jesus was born, the rock where he was raised from the dead. But somehow this still did not feel like the bedrock of my faith.

I had the sense of being shut out. "It is closed," the Russian monk had said, as if making a pronouncement on The Quest itself.

When Mary had stood in front of the doors of the Church of the Holy Sepulchre, they had been closed to her too:

I came with the pilgrims into the outer courtyard of the church. When the Hour of Divine Exaltation came, I struggled to get to the entrance of the church. With the others, I pushed and shoved. I hastened to enter with the crowd. I, the wretched one, was trying, with much toil and affliction, to draw near to the inner temple.

But every time I stepped on the threshold of the door, while all the others entered unhindered, some divine power stopped me and denied me permission to enter. I was pushed back again and again until I found myself alone in the outer courtyard. I decided that this was happening because I was so weak a woman, so I again elbowed my way forward and pressed toward the door. But I labored in vain. When my wretched foot stepped on the threshold, the others were received with no impediment. But I was not received.

When doors appear in myths, they signify that something of spiritual value is contained within. If a door is closed or locked, you know intuitively that it is the hero's job to get through that door. Estés writes, "If there is a secret something, if there is a shadow something, if there is a forbidden something, it needs to be looked into." Mary of Egypt had lived in the open—slept not behind doors but in doorways. She found her own way in or out of things, regardless of welcome. She had run away from home, scraped together a life in Alexandria, forced her way onto that boat.

But now she faced something she could not manipulate or seduce. She heard a powerful "No." The door of the church was, as Estés might put it, a "guard placed in front of a secret," a psychic barrier. In myth, Estés says, a closed door can be a warning: "Don't think too much." "Don't go into the inner temple." "Don't look at your life too closely."

But the closed door is, paradoxically, also the opening of a question. "Asking the proper question is the central action of transformation," Estés writes. A properly shaped question opens the door that had been closed, but it has to be a question that draws you more deeply into your own life. Once you have found this question, you can't go back the way you came. This is indeed what happened to Mary as she stood in the courtyard of the Church of the Holy Sepulchre after everyone else had gone inside and she was alone.

Mary's first attempt—as I can imagine all of ours might be—was to try to force the door open. She pushed and she shoved. She used all of her physical strength to force the barrier aside. She wanted what she wanted. But eventually, force failed her: "I grew weary, no longer able to push and shove (for my body was being beaten by the violence) and I gave in. I withdrew to the corner of the courtyard of the temple. Only then, ever so gradually, did I begin to perceive the cause of my hindrance in seeing the life-giving wood. I became touched in the eyes of my heart."

After so much effort, another possibility emerged. Within herself, she began to perceive an alternative, another story about the "cause of her hindrance." This inner whispering grew into an inner understanding. *I became touched in the eyes of my heart.*

CROSS THE THRESHOLD

1.

There was only one person in the vicinity who appeared to know anything about Mary of Egypt. Dan Koski was an American living in the West Bank and denied a visa to travel outside of it. He agreed to meet me at a coffee shop near the Church of the Nativity, about twelve miles from the Church of the Holy Sepulchre in the West Bank. To meet Dan, I had to pass through the "security wall" followed by what I came to call "trial by taxi driver." After walking through the mazelike checkpoint, I faced a scrum of nearly desperate men who all asked if I needed a ride. Just choosing one of them felt, in itself, like a blind stunt. I would close my eyes, reach out, and end up in a car. Once inside a taxi, a debate ensued. I was accustomed to debating the fare for a taxi, but I wasn't accustomed to debating where the taxi would take me. On the day I went to meet Dan for the first time, the taxi driver I chose from the melee was a gray-haired man named Mahmoud, who said he had once lived in California.

"Nativity Square," I said to him. I had done my research about the cost. "Twenty shekels."

"Thirty," he said. "This time of day, traffic. It is thirty."

"Twenty."

Mahmoud ignored me. "I take you to see Shepherd Fields. Five minutes."

"No thanks," I said. "I have a meeting."

"Five minutes. I take you to Mar Saba."

"No thanks. I have a meeting."

Instead of taking me directly to Nativity Square, he took me to the top of a hill and insisted that I get out and gaze across the desert at the Dead Sea. Then he pointed out the sites.

"There Nativity Church. There the Herodion. In between, Russian Mafia Hotel."

It was a relief to walk into the bright coffee shop and find Dan. An American from Minnesota, he was easy to pick out. Formerly a Lutheran, he had converted to Orthodoxy and had lived in the West Bank for ten years. He was a devotee of Mary of Egypt.

I had only just sat down and ordered tea with mint when Dan looked over my shoulder and said, "I can't believe it." He waved over a woman who had walked in.

"This is Anna," he said to me. "If there was one person in all of Israel that I would have wanted you to meet, this is the one. And I haven't seen her in months."

She was a young woman with long, curly, dark hair, a Greek American who worked for the Greek Orthodox Patriarchate. When I told her about the chapel, she looked puzzled.

"I admit, I've never heard of it," she said, "but I learn new things about this place every day. I'll look into it. Come to my office on Friday."

When Dan returned to our table after talking business with Anna, he began to talk about Mary of Egypt.

"Two of the most revered women in the Judean Desert are Mary of Egypt and Mary the Mother of God," he said. "Mary of Egypt is one of the only female saints in this region from that era who wasn't a wealthy patroness of the church or the mother of another saint.

"But don't be surprised," Dan continued, "if you don't find her in Jerusalem. Remember, she fled from here. She is most powerful in isolated places. Her spirit is in the desert with the monks. She is like the prophet Elijah who received bread in the wilderness. Spiritual communication with her is greatest among the loneliest and most remote of the monks."

He urged me to explore this aspect of Mary of Egypt by going to Mar Saba, an ancient monastery where women were not allowed inside.

"But go to the door anyway," Dan said. "Brother Ephraim is usually there. Tell him you need to see Father Philaret."

As he spoke, I scribbled these instructions in my notebook.

"Here's the essence of the story that Father Philaret will tell you," Dan said. "About a hundred years ago, I believe it was after World War I, a woman came to the monks of Mar Saba dressed as a man. She lived in the community for more than a year. They believe that she was able to do this because she was in spiritual communication with Mary of Egypt. When someone discovered that she was a woman, she fled toward the Jordan River and was last seen by some Bedouins near Jericho. They believe that she crossed over the river and went into the desert. The monks went looking for her, but they never found her. They have maintained her story as a living tradition. Maybe if she really was a saint, her relics will one day be found and brought back to Mar Saba."

We paused around this strange story, lapsing into silence. I had long been fascinated by women hidden as male monks in these late ancient stories. There were several of these in the book that Sophronius's companion wrote, *The Spiritual Meadow*, and there were many more in the book where Mary of Egypt's story is recorded, *Patrologia Graeca*. I felt tenderness both for this unknown woman and for the monks who chased after her, for the way that she ran when she was discovered and felt unwelcome. Who knows what stories lay under this one. In the ancient stories, the woman who attempts this is almost never mocked or hated for her deceit. Her secret is usually discovered at her death, when the monks realize that the holy person they revered is a woman, and they are stunned—you might say bewildered.

Their surprise is akin to Zosimas's surprise when he goes into the desert searching for a holy man and finds instead a holy woman. "What man has surpassed me?" he asks, and the secret answer is that a woman, hidden in the desert, has surpassed him in holiness. The way that the monks chased after her also felt full of love and longing, maybe even the same longing that had driven me all this way across the desert in search of something that might not be found.

"But don't get the wrong idea about monasticism in this region," Dan said, as if he knew my thoughts had gone in quite romantic directions. "People come here all the time looking for the true desert, the place where monks sit in their cells in silence, weaving baskets. They write books on desert spirituality, romanticizing it. That's more of a place in their imagination. The true desert now is a place of overpopulation, poverty, environmental degradation, and political conflict. That's what those who choose the monastic life here face."

He looked at me directly and narrowed his eyes as if interrogating me. Then he asked, "If Mary of Egypt's life has meaning today, what is that meaning?" He had asked the "so what" question. I cringed.

"I don't think I know that yet," I said. "She is pretty elusive."

2.

The next day, my mother got up early for a bus tour to Nazareth. After she left, I laid awake in the predawn, listening to the call to prayer wafting over from the West Bank.

"Find a crack"—these were the words leftover somehow from my now forgotten dreams. In the space between sleeping and waking, I thought of the crack running down the face of the icon of Mary the Mother of

God in the chapel off the courtyard at the Church of the Holy Sepulchre. *You don't need the whole of Jerusalem for The Quest*, I thought. Just find a crack. Maybe, if I couldn't get in to the Chapel of Mary of Egypt, this icon of Mary the Mother of God could stand in for the one that Mary of Egypt had confronted in the courtyard. I decided that I would go back there and behold the cracked Mary.

In the absence of my mother and in the absence of Mary of Egypt, I imagined doing what pilgrims often do: create a route in the direction of their saint and then follow it. Inspired by the Via Dolorosa and the Stations of the Cross, I mentally began to set up my own set of stations that followed the path of Mary of Egypt in Jerusalem. The map of this quest within a quest looked like this:

I. Jaffa Gate, where Mary enters Jerusalem, having trekked from Jaffa with other pilgrims.

II. The ancient marketplace, where Mary would have gone looking for men to have sex with.

III. The courtyard of the Church of the Holy Sepulchre, where Mary was blocked from entering the church.

IV. The icon of Mary the Mother of God, who helped Mary see her life in a new way.

V. The church interior, where Mary went to kiss the "life-giving wood" of the cross.

VI. The Christian quarter of the Old City, where someone gave Mary three coins with which she bought three loaves of bread for her journey.

VII. St. Stephen's Gate, out of which she departed to begin her walk toward the Jordan River.

I took the Palestinian bus into the city. On the bus, I studied the face of the woman who sat in front of me through her reflection in the window. She leaned against the window with her eyes closed. She had all the features of an icon, I thought—a long face that carried some burden, smooth skin, and perfectly sculpted features, with her hair tucked under her hijab. With the dark circles under her eyes, she looked like one of the more tired saints.

Station I: Jaffa Gate

At the Jaffa Gate, I sat on a stone wall and watched the machine gun–carrying soldiers mix in the crowd. There were men in Hasidic dress and women pushing baby strollers and hundreds of tourists. The languages were myriad: Arabic, Hebrew, English, Ukrainian, Russian, Spanish, Polish, Swahili, French. I saw a woman in a leopard-print hijab and a man in a kippah carrying a *lulav*—a combination of palm, myrtle, and willow branches—that was traditional for the start of Sukkoth, the Jewish harvest festival.

Arrival happens before understanding happens, I reminded myself. Mary arrives at the Jaffa Gate on the verge of a transformation that is far beyond her understanding. Everything for her is essentially the same at this moment. She is on the hunt. She is still seeking the same rewards with the same set of eyes. Entering the city with the crowds does not change that. It is business as usual.

When you enter through the Jaffa Gate, there is a strong tug to go with the crowd. Wherever the crowd is going, you go as well. You follow the flow of people as if pulled along by a tide. For Mary, this tide must've been even more powerful, with everyone arriving for the Feast of the Holy Cross. It would've been easy for me to follow the crowd to the Church of the Holy Sepulchre, since this was the general direction of the masses. If I had seen "Mary" on the bus, I didn't see her again here, but I could feel how she would have been drawn into the city, drawn toward her destination that she had no way of perceiving from this place.

Station II: The Ancient Marketplace

I followed a French-speaking family along the cobblestone streets in the direction of the market. The women were dressed as if going to a party. They wore dresses and high-heeled shoes on the uneven streets. One of them even had bright-pink shoes like Cinderella's slippers, which intensified the effect. A woman walked toward me in a T-shirt that said in English, "Fashion is a must."

If this isn't the old self, I thought, *I don't know what is.* Projection and protection of our images of ourselves, the willingness to buy and sell ourselves to get what we want, the willingness to suffer in order to be seen. High heels on cobblestone.

When I got to the actual ruin of the marketplace, it was empty. I walked down the stone steps as if descending into a mythical world. Up above, there was plenty of noise, but down below, my only company was a black cat. I was surrounded by stone ruins—fallen columns and cream-colored stone walls with old doorways and porticos leading nowhere. I could see the orderly Roman stones and the haphazard Byzantine ones set on top, like at Kom el-Dikka.

I had the feeling—for the first time on The Quest—that Mary of Egypt was close by. Maybe this is something like the feeling people get when they walk "where Jesus walked." This was her place, and I felt a chill along my neck.

In these ruins, I could imagine a couple ducking into a doorway for quick sex or someone homeless finding a place to sleep for the night. If prayer had accumulated in the rocks at the Monastery of St. Anthony, here transaction had accumulated—thousands of years of buying and selling of goods and animals that people had piled up in the rocks. Trading and bargaining and bringing what you had to the table. Mary knew transactions well. She had survived on them. Even though the marketplace was empty, I could imagine the energy that brought people from so many different places here at this now blocked crossroads to buy and sell.

Only the old self can be bought and sold. The new one is too fragile, ever emerging. Only the old life can be transformed into an image, crystallized into the self, the ego. The new life can only be lived.

The marketplace crystallized Mary's old life into one word: *transaction*.

On the street above me, I heard a young man call out, "This is the way!" I laughed at the irony. Hadn't I been wondering if this was the way? Apparently it was. I took his voice as encouragement.

Station III: The Courtyard of the Church of the Holy Sepulchre

It doesn't take long to walk from the old Roman marketplace to the Church of the Holy Sepulchre. Once there, I sat down in the outer courtyard on the Crusaders' staircase and again watched the crowd and waited. An English-speaking guide was talking to a group of tourists about the church's history. She had dreadlocks piled up on her head and spoke in an animated way about Helen, the mother of Constantine, who had found the place where Jesus rose from the dead by asking local people. The guide's version was that Helen had starved a local man until he gave up the goods. "At first he didn't want to tell her the location," the guide said. "But after several days without food, well, he changed his mind." She then recited the ways and manners in which the church had been destroyed over the centuries. "It is indeed a miracle that it is still here," she said.

"Come on, guys," she continued. "I thought you understood how things were going here. What do you think happened next? The church was destroyed by an earthquake." These were the last words I heard as the group disappeared inside the doors.

The courtyard was a threshold in the life of Mary of Egypt, a place between the old life and the new one, the old self and the new self. Volatile and dangerous as thresholds can be, they are often guarded by "liminal deities." Every doorway stands in for the threshold between life and death, the overworld and the underworld. Mary stood in just such a place, although according to the story, she did not yet know it. As in myth, her guardian, her benefactor, her "liminal deity" was there to help her.

I thought of the ways that I so often try to make the old life continue to work even after the new one has already presented itself. I want what has worked in the past to keep working. I don't want to have to change what I know, what I've come to have confidence in. As I imagined Mary pushing on the door again and again, I imagined myself, resistant to change, trying to figure out what the trick was so that I didn't have to enter the new territory. Even now, with Ali's cancer, I kept thinking of the time when this would be over, when she would be well again, when we could resume our old life together. I knew that it was a lie. There was no going back, but I kept imagining it nonetheless.

And this time was different for Mary. Maybe she had pushed her way through in the past, but now, for reasons still hidden from her, she could not.

Station IV: The Icon of Mary the Mother of God

Following the inspiration from my dream, I traced my steps back to the cracked icon of Mary the Mother of God. I crossed the courtyard into the coolness of the interior of what I had learned was the Chapel of St. James. This time the chapel was not empty; people were setting up for a ritual in front of the iconostasis at the front. They had placed a beautiful cake with raspberries on a table as if in preparation for a blessing; the doors of the iconostasis were opened, and people had started to gather and sit in the pews.

I slipped past them into the partially closed-off space where the cracked icon stood. I sat in a pew in front of Mary of the Cracked Eye and reviewed this part of Mary of Egypt's story in my head. The first thing that happened—as spiritual understanding dawned on her, as she was "touched in the eyes of her heart"—was a feeling of remorse. She began to "cry and to moan." That was when she saw the icon of Mary, the one that she called *Theotokos*, "God-bearer." Understanding dawned suddenly, and she found herself able to pray and to ask for guidance. She asked for transformation, for the ability to cross the threshold. From this prayer, she "received the fire of faith" and was able to enter the church.

In some ways, it is a mystical scene, founded on the mystery of transformation where another realm of existence breaks through and speaks to the ordinary. But I have long been struck by Mary the Mother of God's silence. While Mary of Egypt prays to the icon, the icon remains still. This scene is not like the ones I was familiar with from later mystics who had long conversations with Jesus or with Mary that they recorded. Mary of Egypt does all the talking; Mary *Theotokos*, none. In that way, this wasn't a mystical conversation at all. Mary of Egypt was ready for a change. The icon of Mary *Theotokos* provided "some kind of assurance"— a sense of consolation, a sense of possibility.

From the other side of the partition, I heard chanting begin in Greek. I smelled the incense and the candle wax. I heard bells ringing. I looked around. The room I was in was half devotional space, half storage space. There was an old pulpit chair and some candleholders stacked in a corner. Everything looked like it had been made in the nineteenth century.

Then I glanced incidentally next to the damaged Mary, and I saw an icon of Mary of Egypt. It was unmistakable. In the painting, a young woman knelt in front of an icon of Mary that looked much like the one that I contemplated. Mary the Mother of God inclined toward Mary of Egypt as if she had just shifted Jesus to the other hip so that she could get a better look at the kneeling woman. Familiar with icons depicting the two Marys, I had never seen an icon of Mary the Mother of God in which she actually turned toward the person viewing her. Mary Green, an iconographer I knew who had made an icon of Mary of Egypt for me, had told me that it is common in Marian iconography for Mary the Mother of God's eyes to follow a viewer around the room. But this actual turning to look was not traditional.

The icon of Mary of Egypt, the first I had seen on the whole quest, was clearly a recent one. The style was contemporary and Greek. Mary of Egypt was pale skinned and modestly dressed. I was startled. Just the other day, I had stood in this same spot, lamenting the fact that there was no icon of Mary of Egypt to be found anywhere. Had I not seen it? Had it not been there? Had I looked past her?

I felt as if I had slipped from the ordinary realm to a magical one. I was being led. It felt as though some part of me had been leaning in and listening while the rest of me jabbered on about being lost and not knowing. I felt I now stood on the boundary between a known and an unknown world.

"Find a crack," the dream had said. And here I was.

Station V: The Church Interior

But even after such a revelation, I was immediately thrown back into my own lack of pious devotion. The next station on Mary's journey involved the True Cross, and I was no closer to feeling its draw than I had been upon first stepping into the church.

In the account of Mary's life that I was following, Mary walked at once into the church after her encounter with the icon. But her attitude was not a triumphant one. The experience had changed her, and she was in awe: "I was overcome then by shivering and amazement. I was confused and trembling. Coming to the door that had been sealed to me, I felt that all the power that had once hindered me, now prepared me to enter. I went in without trouble and once inside the holy of holies, I came to the life-giving vision of the cross. I saw the mysteries of God, who is ready to receive the repentant."

Mary went with everyone else to kiss the remnant of the True Cross. This time, nothing held her back. The "no" had been transformed into a "yes."

I walked out of the chapel and into the bright sunshine of the court-yard and then crossed the threshold myself into the dreamlike interior of the church, with all of its passageways and rooms. I didn't know if remnants of the True Cross were still kept somewhere in the church. If I had been a Greek Orthodox pilgrim, I would have known exactly where to look for them, but I was not.

As a Protestant, I resisted the notion of the True Cross's existence. I remembered the story told in the letters of Egeria, a nun who wrote home to her sisters about her travels in the Holy Land in the fourth century. She reported that someone had bitten off a piece of the True Cross in order to steal it and described how the cross had to be guarded constantly because of these kinds of thieves. I imagined sinking my teeth into the wood of the cross; would that make it feel more real? I knew that there were millions of pieces of the True Cross spread across the Christian world—magically multiplying, magically regenerating, as bishops of the late ancient world had claimed. Reassembled, they would make hundreds if not thousands of True Crosses.

I sat across from the Chapel of Adam, where tradition says that Adam was buried—right under Golgotha so that the Old Man and the New Man could be remembered together in this way. I felt like I was not only inside of a real place (the Church of the Holy Sepulchre in Jerusalem) but also inside a version of my own mind that was full of closed doors and endless passageways, blockages and unexpected openings. The church felt like it could expand and contract as if in a Borges story. It was full of half-finished things—broken, incomplete, always in process. New. Old.

I decided to find monks to ask about the Chapel of Mary of Egypt again. Maybe Anna would come through on Friday; maybe she would not. In the meantime, I shouldn't be cowardly. I would ask as many monks in as many different styles of hat and robe as I could.

Even as I thought this, a light went on behind a closed door in front of me. In a few minutes, this closed door opened, and I saw a monk sitting behind a desk in a black robe wearing a small, square black hat. I went to the door, and the man immediately looked down at his paperwork. I noticed that his hands were burled and swollen, almost to the point of not being usable. When I asked, in English, about the Chapel of Mary of Egypt, he shook his head as though he didn't understand, so I tried again in Russian, in French, and then in my tiny bit of Arabic, *Miryam al Masreya*. To this, he shook his head and waved me away.

I went back out into the main area in search of more monks. I asked a Franciscan monk in English.

"I think the Copts have it," he said.

I went to the small Coptic chapel behind the Edicule. I recognized the Coptic monks from the style of their caps, like Father Lucas's.

"The Greeks have it," one monk responded confidently. "And it is only open one day a year."

The Armenians, the Greeks, the Copts, the Franciscans, the Russians— I felt like I was in one of those cartoons where Wile E. Coyote encounters a sign pointing in ten different directions at once. I walked out into the courtyard discouraged, and I saw a boy with a T-shirt that said "Difficult" broken apart and configured in many different ways. I saw a monk I thought was Greek Orthodox and approached him to ask about the chapel.

"The Copts have it," he said.

Station VI: The Christian Quarter

When Mary came out of the church after kissing the True Cross, she returned to the icon and continued her conversation with it: "'Now where you command, lead,' she said to Mary, *Theotokos*. 'Be the teacher that leads me on the road to repentance.' As I said this, I heard from a distance a voice cry out, 'If you cross the Jordan, you will find a beautiful rest.' I heard the voice and I believed that it was for me. I cried out to the *Theotokos*, 'Queen, do not forsake me,' and having cried out these words, I went out from the courtyard of the church and started walking away."

Be teacher. Be queen. The icon didn't speak back. Mary the Mother of God didn't climb down out of the iconostasis and give Mary a hug. Even the voice she heard from a distance could have been instructions for anyone, just as I had heard someone call out, "This is the way!" Like so many spiritual conversations, this was an interior conversation. Yet something compelled Mary to trust what she heard—and not only to trust it but to stake her life on it.

Mary was a stranger in this country. She didn't know where the Jordan was. Her decision to take these words for herself, even though she heard them "from a distance," seems just shy of an act of desperation. Her life had suddenly taken a different course. She was gripped by something she called "the fire of faith," but her next steps were unclear.

She went outside, and as if in a fairy tale, she was given three coins. With the three coins, she bought three loaves of bread. She asked the person from whom she bought the bread, "Where is the road that leads to the Jordan?" He pointed in that direction, and she headed to the gate that led out of the city.

The moment of transformation is an intensely vulnerable one. Mary was a stranger. Even if, to this point, she would not have called herself a pilgrim, she had become one. She didn't know much about where she was. None of that had mattered because her old ways had sufficed. But now that her previous way of life had been abandoned, she faced an emptiness.

On any pilgrimage, Dan Koski said later as we talked about the meaning of the three coins, you reach the end of your rope quickly. You've exposed yourself to radically different terrain.

"You might not know the languages and the customs of the people around you and have to ask questions from people you would otherwise not speak to," he explained. "Your body is adjusting to new climates, time zones, diet. On the actual pilgrimage trail, money is spent and not earned. Your traveling possessions are being put to stress tests and often need to be replaced after being broken, waterlogged, stolen, lost, or accidentally discarded. You're tired and homesick and dealing with new social and cultural dynamics. On a pilgrimage, you have to be cognizant of blessings that come your way."

Mary, Dan guessed, was probably a pretty thick-skinned woman. She had seen a lot; she had been through a lot. She had been hurt, it is safe to guess, a lot. But true pilgrimage breaks a person down. It disrupts old certainties. It demands new ways of being, seeing, and acting. Pilgrimage is the true and often ugly story of meeting an end in yourself, of having the myth of your self-sufficiency shattered.

Until this moment, Mary's life had been built on her ability to manipulate others to gain what little advantage she could. Now she had been given a purpose and a direction. She knew which way to go. But none of her usual means for getting there were available. Here at this end, which is also a beginning, coins appear. To accept them, she has to bow her neck. She trades nothing for these coins. Not beauty. Not desire. Not sex. Not work. They come free. One scholar suggests that Mary had perhaps already taken on the persona of an *amma*, a female ascetic of the desert, and the fact that someone gives her the coins is evidence of that transformation. "Take this, my mother," a man says—even though, for once, she has asked for nothing.

After an encounter like the one Mary had with the *Theotokos*, she was receptive, open in a new way. Before, she might have been grasping, greedy, desperate to get what everyone else had. But afterward, she gave herself no choice but to trust.

As I walked out of the courtyard, I tried to locate myself in relation to the gate. I laughed as I stood among the olivewood knickknacks, shawls, candles, and icons, thinking that the most miraculous part of the story of Mary of Egypt is imagining that you could be in the Old City and someone would give you money instead of take your money.

I didn't buy three loaves of bread as I made my way toward the gate. I just walked, taking in the sights and sounds, wondering what it would have felt to walk this way after having abandoned your old life. I had walked the most direct route that I could find from the courtyard of the Church of the Holy Sepulchre to St. Stephen's Gate. There was nowhere on that route to stop. Everyone was moving all the time. I passed bakeries and juice stands. I passed the Islamic Industrial Orphanage School. *Even*, I thought, *if Mary of Egypt were in the midst of a radical change of life, everything around her would have stayed the same.* Jerusalem would still have been, as Jerome described it, "a terribly crowded city which has its government buildings, its barracks, its prostitutes, troupes of actors, clowns and all the rest." That had not changed. She had changed.

Station VII: St. Stephen's Gate

At St. Stephen's Gate (now usually called Lions' Gate), the road opens out from the city, weaving around the Mount of Olives toward the east. The road going east is called Jericho Road, and it leads toward the Jordan River, a distance of about fifteen miles. I walked out of the gate into the intensity of the concrete-reflected sun on the other side. In front of me was the Mount of Olives, and I looked up toward it, trying to find a path through it with my eyes. The sky here was brighter, bigger, more insistent. This was the way that Mary took toward the Jordan.

I was at the end of my stations. I had come as close to Mary of Egypt in geography as I was distant in time—to touch, to hear, to smell. I had followed one who had made sure to erase her footsteps. I had taken it upon myself to gesture toward the unknown by way of the known, and perhaps this is the essence of pilgrimage.

We might not know if Mary actually existed, but we know the marketplace, we know the courtyard, we know St. Stephen's Gate. Maybe we even know, inside ourselves, what Mary knew: forces beyond us are working for our transformation all the time, and we are being asked to walk through new doors, to grow bigger eyes, to reach toward something we don't understand.

Augustine of Hippo once wrote, "When people are hungry, they stretch out toward something; while they are stretching, they are enlarged; while they are enlarged, they become capacious, and when they have become capacious enough, they will be filled in due time." In the city of Jerusalem, Mary stretched toward what she could not understand. She stepped over the next threshold and turned her face to the desert.

I walked back toward the bus, smelling sage and orange water and bread.

OPEN THE DOOR

1.

In the middle of the night, I woke up hot and panicked. I was again in a stone city with arches and passageways and courtyards. *Where am I? What city?* I searched through the city, looking for something but not finding it. From somewhere within the dream, the answer came: "You are in Jerusalem." But then I fell asleep again and the panic returned. Then again the answer: "Jerusalem." I woke up again and was awake for a long time waiting for the call to prayer.

When the call to prayer began, I got up and opened the balcony door to listen.

I thought about the evening before. At dinner, I'd had a conversation with Amanda, a woman staying at the retreat center to work on her thesis about the Catholic theologian Karl Rahner. I had told her about my quest, and she'd looked at me, deeply puzzled.

"The last time I heard anything about Mary of Egypt was in undergrad," she said. There she had learned that Mary of Egypt was a legend, a story the monks made up for the edification of other monks. That made the idea of "following in her footsteps" strange. Amanda was careful not to use the word *naive*, but I felt the term between us. What could conjure up my interest in a mere wisp of a seventh-century edifying tale and take me so far from home?

In the darkness of the morning, I thought about this category of "as if" that I had so thoroughly embraced in order to undertake this journey. I walked in Mary's footsteps "as if" she existed. I lived "as if" Ali was not going to die. It wasn't a game of pretend. "As if" didn't mean not true; it meant that I had consented to accept certain things as unknowns, even perhaps unknowable. But it also meant admitting the role of the imagination in the enterprise of being alive. "The first step for any pilgrim lands not on the road, but somewhere in the imagination," historian Georgia Frank writes. I had pretty aptly demonstrated that the imagination does not abandon the pilgrim on the road but continues to shape the path.

I thought of David Jasper, of his insistence that Mary's story could not be walked, that she could not be followed. I felt a longing to be writing about someone like Karl Rahner, a systematic theologian who had actually lived, who had written books, whose words could be researched and interpreted. So concrete, so doable.

I had embraced an "as if," a "waking dream," and the twists and turns had ended up being dreamlike. Like the city in my dreams, I found myself walking passages and asking again and again, "Where am I?"

It was my mother's last day in Israel. I wondered if she wanted to see the Dead Sea Scrolls or visit Yad Vashem. I was game to give up The Quest for a day if she just wanted to be a tourist. She looked at me as puzzled as Amanda had been the night before. "Why would I want to do that?"

Anna had told us that Friday would be a good day to find her at the Greek Orthodox Patriarchate, so we decided to start the day there. We made our way to the Jaffa Gate like pros, but once we turned up Greek-Catholic Patriarchate Street, we were as lost as we had ever been. We found many closed doors with the symbol of the Greek Orthodox Patriarchate on them but no way in. At long last, a maintenance man looked at us with some sympathy. We mentioned Anna's name, and he took us through a set of courtyards, stairs, and hallways to an office door. We knocked, but she was not there.

This kind of seeking and not finding is par for the course for the pilgrim, but it is still exhausting. I had not set out with the expectation that doors would magically open and the meaning and purpose of The Quest would become magically clear. At the beginning of *The Snow Leopard*, Peter Matthiessen's account of his quest to see this elusive creature in the highlands of Nepal, his teacher Eido Roshi says to him, "Expect nothing." This is apt advice, no doubt, and the orientation I embraced. But it is not easy advice to live day after day. Matthiessen never does see a snow leopard. I imagine that he spent a lot of hours on his long hike planning the chapter of the book he would write when he at last sees this mystical being, the enlightenment he would receive, the rare beauty, the glimpse of that life beyond life. He never got to write that chapter. The chapter he wrote instead was about how the journey itself was the meaning.

Here we were outside another closed door, and the "precision and openness and intelligence of the present," as another Buddhist teacher put it, was as elusive as Mary of Egypt.

The day was hot. Our tempers were tried. The sun was relentless. Anna was absent. The maintenance man offered to let us use his phone, and we called her. She agreed to meet us later at a trendy café near the Jaffa Gate. It wasn't much; we were Hansel and Gretel on a trail of crumbs.

"What does she look like?" my mother asked as we sat at a table in the crowded café waiting for Anna.

I looked around. "She has long, dark, curly hair just like every other woman in this café," I said.

Anna, the Greek American New Yorker, looked every bit the part of a trendy Israeli. She made her way through the café toward us with a coffee in one hand and her phone in another. She looked harried.

"I tried to WhatsApp and cancel," she said. "But when you didn't answer, I just rearranged my schedule." It was true that our phones worked only in rare environments in Israel.

She set her phone down next to her and glanced at it. "OK," she said, gathering herself. "About this chapel." My mother and I leaned in. "Yes. It exists. The patriarchate owns it, and the archbishop has the key. He will meet you there. Maybe tomorrow."

After the rigmarole at the Church of the Holy Sepulchre, this answer was strikingly straightforward.

"I'll WhatsApp you when the bishop is headed to the office and he has time to meet you. I just don't know when exactly."

Then Anna relaxed, as if her mission had been accomplished. We sipped our coffees, and she told us her story of coming to Jerusalem and of believing that the Greek Orthodox Patriarchate was a place from which she might do some good.

That night, I walked my mother to the shuttle bus after supper. She had been the perfect traveling companion: intrepid, steady, and indefatigable on The Quest. She had not looked at me, not even once, as if this were a crazy waste of her mother's inheritance. I was sorry that we would not cross the threshold of the chapel together.

2.

The next day, I did nothing. The air smelled like a hot summer day in South Dakota, a combination of rose bushes and humidity. I sat in the retreat center library and read. I asked Jacqueline, the French librarian, if there were any books about Mary of Egypt in the library—anything even tangentially related—and maybe if there was anything about the Feast of the True Cross. She brought me some French and Spanish legends of Mary of Egypt and book after book about various Christian groups jockeying for position in the Old City. I read about Russians and Ethiopians and Armenians. I read about how Russian peasants used to appoint one person in their home parish—usually an old woman—to make the trek to the Holy Land and bring back "holy fire" from the Church of the Holy Sepulchre. I read that now there are Learjets parked on the tarmac in Tel Aviv ready to carry planeloads of holy fire back to Russia.

Once again, reading in the library, as if from nowhere, the tears started. I remembered a prayer that I had copied down in my notes from one of the desert fathers, St. Gregory the Theologian. I had shared it with Ali because I knew she would like it.

O God,
who pours out mercy and kindness,
who ever invites me,
the one who ever turns away from you . . .
as you did in the past
with the rock in the desert,
make my stony and petrified heart
gush forth fountains of tears.

This is what it felt like: I walked over rocks, and little springs gushed up. I cried almost every time I sat down, every time Ali and the old life appeared. The old life planned to wash itself away in tears.

I was in the library when Anna's text arrived:

Amy, Bishop Isidoros said u can come to the office in the Holy Sepulchre at 2:30. He's finishing in the courts, so he's guessing around 2–2:30 he'll be there. It's right through the door on the right side, under Golgotha. Then there's a little office door with glass windows.

This was the same office near where I stood when the light went on, I thought. This is where the monk with the arthritic hands and I had had our multilingual failure.

Suddenly I was nervous. What if something went wrong at the last minute? What if the bishop got delayed in the courts or the roof caved in by the time I got there? What if they changed their minds and decided not to bother with an American on a quest? What if there was yet another misunderstanding and I was headed to the chapel of the wrong Mary?

I got up from the library and ran back to my room to put on a skirt. The irony was not lost on me: attempting to cloak myself in modesty in pursuit of the tradition's least modest saint. But I didn't want to give them any reason to reject me. I felt as though the door had cracked open, and I had only a moment to put my foot in before it closed again.

At the church, the office door was open, and inside were three men dressed in long black robes. One of them was the same man who had been at the desk before, who now sat on a gold-covered couch. Another stood up when I walked in, retrieved his keys from inside his round hat, and went out. The third sat behind the desk. He had a gentle face and a long black beard. He looked young and lively, like someone you would like to have a beer with.

When I introduced myself and said that Anna had sent me, the most extraordinary thing happened. The men smiled. Warmly.

"Welcome," the man behind the desk said. He gestured for me to sit on the couch and said something to the other man, who brought me a glass of lemonade. I thought of something that one of the people at Tantur had said the evening before at dinner: "If you want to find something, ask the women." I could see that Anna's name here was like a key to a door.

Then we sat in silence for several minutes. I thought we were waiting for the bishop, so I said nothing.

Finally the youngest man cleared his throat. "So you want to see the chapel?"

"Yes," I said.

Another silence drew out awkwardly. "May I ask," I said at last, "what is your name?"

"Isidoros," he said.

I blushed. The bishop. He was the person I thought we were waiting for. Wasn't he supposed to be wearing some imposing cape or a hat taller than everyone else's hat? Instead, this quiet, cheerful, kind, simple man seemed awkward about something, but I couldn't tell what it was.

"Well." He cleared his throat again. "So we don't exactly know where the key to the chapel is. I have to go look for it."

"When was the last time it was open?" I asked.

"Many, many years ago," he said. "Perhaps fifty or sixty. Perhaps you would like to venerate the True Cross while I go look for it?"

The True Cross was here? The key to the chapel was missing? All around me were new signs and wonders—clues for The Quest.

He showed me to a small room where remnants of the cross—bits of "life-giving vision," as Mary of Egypt called them—had been placed behind a glass panel on a stand so that people could bend over it and kiss the glass. In this same room were the relics of Sophronius himself and the relics of Anthony of Crete, who wrote the liturgy that kept Mary of Egypt's story alive in the Greek and Russian Orthodox churches.

Once the bishop left to look for the key, I walked around with wonder. Here I was, surrounded by physical aspects of Mary of Egypt—those who had written about her, the bits of the cross that she had perhaps herself venerated on that day. Presumably these were the things I had come to Jerusalem to find. "Reverence the place and learn from what you see," Cyril of Jerusalem had exhorted the pilgrim.

A group of Greek Orthodox pilgrims came in and stood in a line in order to venerate and kiss the glass. They also kissed the glass over the relics of various saints with practiced ease. They had none of my Protestant angst about physical gestures, none of my performance anxiety. I watched them and thought of the way that Mary of Egypt had entered the place where the True Cross was kept: "I went through the door with-out trouble and once inside the holy of holies, I came to the life-giving vision of the cross. I saw the mysteries of God, who is ready to receive the repentant. Throwing myself on the earth and kissing that holy ground, I then ran outside again to my benefactor, the one who had agreed to help me."

I didn't throw myself on the earth and kiss the ground. Instead, after the pilgrims left, I bent my lips awkwardly toward the wooden remnant under the glass and wondered about closed doors that open.

When Bishop Isidoros returned, he held two enormous iron keys in his hands. My sense of being in a fairy tale intensified. Keys like this, if they appeared in a dream, would be the sign of an important secret about to be unlocked.

I followed Bishop Isidoros out into the bright courtyard, and he went directly to the smaller of the two doors that I had wondered about on my first day. Just as the internet had said, the chapel was directly under the Chapel of the Franks. He tried the first key and it didn't work. Then he tried the second, and the little metal door—like something from Alice in Wonderland—creaked open.

The walls of the chapel were made of rough stone, and there was a small window with a metal frame above the door that cast a pattern of sun on the dirt floor.

On one end of the small room stood a mostly empty iconostasis with one icon of Mary the Mother of God holding Jesus. Under this icon, a sign in a mix of Greek and Old Church Slavonic noted the person who gave the icon and the year it was given, 1843. Above this were smaller icons of scenes from Jesus's life: birth, temple blessing, baptism, the raising of Lazarus, and several empty spaces. Everything again had a nineteenth-century appearance.

On the other end of the chapel were strewn construction materials: smooth pieces of stone, some mortar, a few tools, and a lot of dust.

"There is a plan for renovation," the bishop said as he picked up an icon lying inside the iconostasis and dusted it off. He propped it up.

There was no sign of Mary of Egypt anywhere. I wondered if the icon that I had seen across the courtyard in the Chapel of St. James had come from this chapel and been moved when it closed.

"Does anyone ever ask about this chapel?"

Bishop Isidoros shook his head and smiled a little sadly.

I thought about Dan's question: If Mary of Egypt has meaning for today, what is that meaning? And I thought about Dan's admonition: don't be surprised if she is not in Jerusalem.

The whole of the Church of the Holy Sepulchre is, in a way, a monument to emptiness: the empty tomb of Jesus. People have come here for thousands of years to mark the space where a body was not. "He is not here," an angel tells Mary Magdalene on the morning of the resurrection in the Gospel of Matthew. All that remains is an empty space. The church's chapels and marble, its gold, its art, its many and various monuments from different moments in time are collected to remember an absence—a life-giving mystery, Mary of Egypt might say.

I imagined that the people who put this chapel here wanted a place to remember Mary as an icon of repentance. They created the chapel as a place to lay down their own sins, where they could place their own lives in a trajectory of forgiveness. That need had somehow disappeared over the course of time—or at least, the expression of that need in this space. The chapel was closed. The door was locked. The key was lost. The history of the chapel turned into liquid time. I had appeared as a way to remember what had been forgotten—or to remember that it had been forgotten. Was I the last in a long line of pilgrims grown ever sparser over time or the first in a tradition, being born right under my feet?

I left Bishop Isidoros in front of the chapel feeling grateful and sad and even vulnerable, as if the emptiness of that space had opened an emptiness in me—one that I had to carry carefully, almost protectively.

Anything in the process of becoming has to become empty. Die and become, Goethe had said. But he left out what happens in the middle, in the between. The old life has to be released, and in the middle of that releasing, there might just be an empty chapel, a place to remember and a place to forget, a place to lay down the past at a broken altar and allow what had been to liquefy, to empty, to let go.

The great gift that Bishop Isidoros gave me, besides his gentle and kind self, was the gift of seeing the chapel in the midst of transition. He didn't hide its vulnerable betweenness. He didn't have to take the time to find the key, to expose something as vulnerable as the between. He could have said, like the first monk, "It is closed." But he didn't. He opened the door and allowed me to see into a passing away and a becoming that was fragile enough not yet to be known.

When the self steps away from the past and toward the future, it steps toward the unknown. The old self has habits and patterns that the new one doesn't. The Chapel of Mary of Egypt was in the midst of just such a transition. What it will become, when it will become aren't known. That not knowing is vulnerable, and as I walked to the end of the courtyard, I felt soft and tender toward it.

A man stopped me. I recognized him from my many forays as one of the doorkeepers who spend their days in the courtyard. Tradition holds that these keepers of the sepulchre are Muslim. That allows them to be neutral in the battles between many and various Christian sects that have a claim on the space.

"He is our bishop," the man said, gesturing back to the place where I had left Bishop Isidoros.

"Yes," I said.

"He is a good man. A great man," the man continued. "He helps everyone!"

I thought of the chain of affection of which I was now a part: Dan to Anna to the bishop to this man. That love had been graciously extended to me, a stranger, and had allowed me to see into the fleeting, unsettled moment of becoming.

As I walked toward the bus, I thought how different this sensation was from the one that had possessed me in my earlier search for the chapel when everyone I asked claimed the chapel in some way for someone else: "The Copts have it," "The Greeks have it." I had the sense of the spaces being divvied up between entities, but when I entered the chapel, I encountered a profound emptiness.

In the Gospel of John, after the resurrection, Jesus says to his disciples, "Do not hold on to me." Zosimas said something similar of Mary of Egypt. As he kissed her feet, he noted that he "could not hold for long she who would not be held."

3.

I could see now something about myself and about the pilgrimage. Pilgrimage offers the intense pleasure of seeing the world as a collection of signs pointing the way. You have to hone your skills of perception, cultivate the mysteries of beholding, attend relentlessly to what the "intelligence of the present" is telling you. I had come on a pilgrimage in order to transform the whole of my life into signs. I had to lean in close and listen. All the mysterious whisperings, dream images, and fleeting impulses became, under the conditions of pilgrimage, a method, a life-encompassing prayer: take me, lead me, show me.

I had come here to teach myself to pay attention to the smell of roses and hot pavement, to what messages might be available in the birds calling "habibti" from the branches of olive trees. When you live by signs, the world comes more fully alive, imbued with a spiritual sense. I crave the making of every detail into significance, no matter how small. I collect trinkets that I find on sidewalks and pick up pennies. I need to know the names of stalks of grass, and I feel delight when I learn that this plant is hibiscus and that one is oleander. But on a pilgrimage, this attention is further heightened, and each detail has the potential to point the way.

I had come this way so that I could offer everything—my time, my money, my life—to The Quest for the Wild Woman. I would like to be able to undertake this alchemy—this transformation of life into signs— all the time at home. But as a pilgrim, it was demanded of me.

What is a Wild Woman after all but a person who has learned to read the landscape and interpret its most intimate traces?

PART III
PALESTINE
AND JORDAN

Expect nothing. Live frugally on surprise.

—Alice Walker

The wilderness that everyone fears has become a great place of refuge,
where assistance flows from their bones to all creation.

—ancient Syriac poem

GET LOST

1.

Stepping through the back gate of the retreat center, I was suddenly aware of the number of dead pine needles under my feet. I saw thick rose hips on the rose bushes where before I had seen only roses. The oranges on the orange trees were more orange than they had been just yesterday, and the leaves in the blackberry hedges showed signs of yellowing. All day long I had seen women out beneath the olive trees collecting olives. I felt the sensations of autumn in a climate far different from the one I was used to. In the mountains of Colorado, a change in the air is usually the first sign of fall. Here the air was still hot, but color and texture announced a change in season.

My husband was coming to accompany me on the last and most physically demanding part of the pilgrimage. We planned to hike from Bethlehem to Jericho in an approximation of Mary's trip from Jerusalem to Jericho on the old Roman Road. According to the *Life*, Mary covered the distance in a day: "And learning which gate of the city leads out in that direction, I set off running. I took to the journey weeping. By asking along the way, I drew near the place by the end of the day. (I guess it had been the third hour of the day when I saw the Cross.) As the sun was setting, I reached the Church of John the Baptist situated near the Jordan."

I knew people who had done this—left Jerusalem and hiked to Jericho in a day—but things had become more complicated politically. The Wadi Qelt—the direct route between Jerusalem and Jericho—crisscrossed Israeli and Palestinian lands, and when I researched it, I had difficulty finding a guide who could take us that way. Instead, I had found an organization called Walk in Palestine, and they had arranged a longer route through the most desertlike part of the Judean Desert, joining Mary's path about midway through Wadi Qelt and continuing along Wadi Qelt to Jericho and the Jordan River.

Walking some portion of this pilgrimage felt imperative. In writing about traditional pilgrimage, Victor Turner notes that the pilgrim "earns more merit . . . by ignoring modern means of transportation." This merit comes, in part, through humility. You expose yourself to the elements; you let your feet get sore. You acknowledge who you are apart from air-conditioned buses and smooth roads from one place to another; you add effort.

But I wasn't after merit. There was no one keeping score, no one totaling my points. Most people at home and all along the way had given me puzzled looks like Amanda's, so merit was not available anyway.

What I was looking for was a change in pace. When we enter old stories, George Steiner writes, we need to be "slowed down, bewildered and barred in our reading so that we may be driven deep." Walking was a deep, slow form of reading the text, entering the story just as I entered the landscape. It was easy for me, working as I did with all the resources of the internet and university libraries, to think I knew things before I had even encountered them, to think I understood something merely because I had information about it. But walking would offer me a different form of teaching.

I hadn't figured out how to walk Mary's route in Egypt, and Tel Aviv to Jerusalem had likewise baffled me from a distance, but now at last the text told me, more or less, where to put my feet, and I was determined to do it.

It was going to be hot. I told Diana, a woman at the front desk of the retreat center, that I worried it would be too hot to walk from Bethlehem to Jericho. She reassured me, "Don't worry! We always say that the weather changes now. We call it 'Cross Weather,' because it is the Feast of the Holy Cross, and that is when it becomes fall."

But an Israeli American woman I had met stared at me and squinted. "I worry for you," she said.

I went to evening prayer that night still sweaty. I had just come from Bethlehem, where I had once again been through "trial by taxi driver." This time my driver had insisted that I pay 150 shekels for the privilege of a trip to the refugee camp. I had been trying simply to go from Nativity Square to the checkpoint. When I said "No thank you. The checkpoint is fine," he told me about a surgery that one of his children had to have and how he hadn't had a single fare all day.

I observed an instinct in myself to "help," even if he was lying to me. I negotiated the price down to ninety shekels and still was driven where I did not want to go. Hot and tired and frustrated, I found myself at the Dheisheh Refugee Camp, where I saw graffitied walls and barbed wire. I saw the UN distribution point for food and the UN school. Despite the bullying, I admired the cab driver for taking upon himself the role of ambassador to misery and possibly empathy—for trying to teach visitors the true nature of where they were while they glanced at historical and biblical sites.

2.

I had gone to Bethlehem to meet with Dan again at Casa Nova. This time he urged me to consider the paths that Mary of Egypt didn't choose. She could have, he suggested, become an abbess in a monastery. A lot of abbesses and abbots, along with monks and nuns, had checkered pasts. Repentance was highly valued in that society. She might have been able to find an in, and once her story became known, she might have risen in the ranks. It might have been tempting for her, after her life at the mercy of men in power, to have had men come to her and ask for her blessing. The empress Theodora had taken a path similar to this one. She had lived as an actress and a prostitute before converting to Christianity and eventually marrying the emperor Justinian.

Or Mary could have fallen prey to what Dan called the Jerusalem syndrome. People with badly damaged lives come to Jerusalem in hopes that the city's magic will work on them. When they notice that this doesn't happen, that they are still themselves and have not been healed, the knowledge can be so devastating that they go a little bit crazy. There was no small number of these people in Jerusalem both then and now. They've sacrificed everything to get to the Holy Land in hopes that it will heal them. But the work of real transformation is much harder. It requires something different from the magical thinking that the holy sites inspire: decades of trial and error, self-correction, help from others. Mary of Egypt herself gives no rosy portrait as she struggles in the desert with her old life and her longing for transformation:

Believe me . . . seventeen years I wandered in this desert, fighting with fierce beasts of wordless desires. Whenever I attempted to partake of food, I desired the meats and fishes of Egypt. I most desired wine to drink. For when I had been in the world, I often indulged in a great deal of wine. But here, I did not even have water to taste. I burned dreadfully, and there was no trial I did not bear. To my mind came all the brothel songs unexpectedly, troubling me dreadfully, and seducing me to sing the odes of demons, whose songs I had learned. Immediately, I wept and beat my breast with my hands.

Mary's struggle, even after she had departed for the wilderness, even after she had found her teacher, was not over. It had only just started as she confronted herself—who she had been, the truth about the comforts on which she had relied, the way her brain was wired. Her transformation in the wilderness required her to face all of this not in a moment but over seventeen years.

The other thing about Jerusalem, Dan said, is that everyone wants to plant a flag. Everyone wants to make a claim on the city. Jerusalem is a place where important people constantly appear—politicians, religious leaders, celebrities. If you stay in the city, you might have the opportunity to sit at the table of power, to learn the inside scoop on important things, to touch the cloak of history. This was true even for ascetic women, who might have seemed like the outsiders of the outsiders, on the far edge of things. For many ascetic women, the path of asceticism was not as much surrendering status as it was gaining a kind of status rarer and more rarefied than marriage.

But Mary did not choose any of these. She did not ask for instant healing. She did not go in search of power. She quickly left the city and ran away from whatever rewards it might have offered. She took the path of obscurity and undertook the hard labor of transformation. In fact, she chose an obscurity so complete that it is likely we might never have heard of her.

The kind of provision that Mary received for her journey—the three coins turned into three loaves of bread—was the opposite of the Jerusalem syndrome. In that case, a person makes a demand: "I have come this far. I have sacrificed this much, you have to heal me!" But in Mary's case, she is offered, without asking, just enough to get from point A to point B.

My plan was to follow Mary out into the desert—to smell, taste, and feel what obscurity might have awaited her. Dan reminded me to stop by the ancient monastery of Mar Saba and ask for Father Philaret, as it was on the way out of Bethlehem toward the Wadi Qelt. He also urged me, before I left Jerusalem, to make my way to Bethany. Bethany is a city between Jerusalem and Jericho in the West Bank, behind the wall.

"Mary would certainly have passed that way," he said, as she ran out of Jerusalem. But he also wanted me to see what modern asceticism looked like—the unromanticized part of the desert. There are no hermits in Bethany, but there are people who live in the midst of the conflict that now dictates life in these parts. Dan reminded me that these monastics lived the struggle, the poverty, the environmental distress of the land.

3.

The next day, as my husband's plane was scheduled to arrive in the evening, I started early at the Mount of Olives to find my way to Bethany. I had asked several people how to get there and received conflicting information from each of them. I'd consulted Google Maps only to get more confused. I would make my own way.

Here is something that Mary and I have in common after all: we both "rush off" to places without a clear idea of how to get there. My day, as it transpired, was considerably less successful than Mary's.

Bethany—now called al-Eizariya—is a city cut off by the wall. Once I had taken a bus out through East Jerusalem and gotten off, I quickly found the wall. I could not find any checkpoint to get through the wall. I walked and walked in a no man's land where there were no people of any kind, no cars, no traffic. I knew I must be going the wrong way, but I couldn't bring myself to turn around.

"Travel is a kind of doorway by which we leave reality to enter into a previously unexplored reality that is like a dream," Guy de Maupassant wrote. I did feel once again like I had landed in a dream. The wall loomed on one side, with gated land on the other. I could not find my way through, back to habitation where I could start my journey over. At last, I saw a small open gate on the opposite side of the wall, and I went through it. I walked through a grove of olive trees with no way out. Finally I saw a monastery building and heard voices—male voices—speaking a language I did not recognize. I saw a sign that said "Passionist Roman Catholic Monastery." I almost cried when I reached the porch and rang the doorbell. After a long time, a monk stuck his head out of the window.

"I am lost," I said. "I am wondering whether you could open your gate and let me out."

"Where you go?" asked the monk from the window.

"I am trying to go to Bethany, al-Eizariya. I got lost."

"The checkpoint is around," he said, gesturing in the opposite direction I had come. He let me out of the gate with a buzzer, and I kept walking.

Eventually, I did indeed get to Bethany—by taxi. Then I was still lost. After more wandering, I found my way to the school to which Dan had pointed me.

The ascetic that he had wanted me to meet was Sister Martha, a German woman who runs the school. She converted to Eastern Orthodoxy when she was young, against the will of her parents. She joined the church formally at twenty-one and by twenty-six had discerned a monastic vocation. Her mother had told her, "When you became Orthodox, I thought the worst thing that could happen to you was that you would marry a priest and have ten children. What I wouldn't give for those children now!" But no one was more surprised than she when she felt led to the Holy Land and then led to the school. Running a school was not her idea of the ideal monastic vocation.

"If you joined a monastery where they made books," she said while we sat on kindergarten-sized chairs in the school and sipped coffee with cardamom, "you would learn everything about book making. If the monastery raised animals or painted icons, you would learn everything about animals or icons." Then she paused with a look of good humor and sort of amazement on her face. "But books are silent. Icons are silent. Even animals, after you feed them, are silent. Children are not silent. It is very difficult to figure out how to live a monastic life in this environment."

"So how do you?" I asked.

"It is like walking on a knife's edge," she said. "At every moment, you have the difficulty and the pain of taking the next step. You have to discern carefully how to engage this person or that problem because every moment is an opportunity to move closer to God or farther away. The slightest hint of pride erases the work you've done or the spiritual progress you might have made. But," she went on, "the love and mercy of God are also abundant, and you can see God's work everywhere."

"Thank you for coming," Sister Martha said as I was leaving. "I know it is difficult to get here. We sometimes feel so cut off. Sometimes even the internet doesn't work, and I have to wander around the school looking for a signal to send an email, so I don't always answer quickly."

I headed back to Jerusalem on a bus, through checkpoints and walls. Four times that day, buses I was on were searched by soldiers. I could feel the mute rage of the people around me as the soldiers arrived on the bus, sometimes chatting on their cell phones. I could feel the helplessness as teenagers were removed with no explanation. I could feel my own anxiety heightened with each successive stop until it felt like conflict between Palestinians and Israelis had become a part of me and I had become a part of it. I wanted out of this country with its barbed wire and walls and machine guns. But I knew that that barbed wire and walls and machine guns were every bit as much a part of my own country as they were a part of Israel. The logics were the same. The materials were the same. I wasn't experiencing someone else's culture. I was experiencing my own—from the other side of perhaps only barely less visible walls.

GO INTO THE DEEPER DESERT

1.

Our first day in the Judean Desert ended on a bench looking out over hills empty of vegetation and human life. Though I had never been here, this was the landscape that had formed my understanding of Mary of Egypt. In an icon of Mary of Egypt that Mary Green had made for me and that sat on my windowsill at home, Mary's hands are open in a gesture of prayer, and her gaze is toward a blue, blue sky. She stands in a wild place like this one with no hint of civilization around her.

Some time before leaving on this trip, I had started bringing my icon little gifts from the out-of-doors. I brought the Mary of my icon an acorn, a daisy, and the nub of a poppy, whose desiccated center was now a star. I became especially obsessed with bringing her things that were at the end of their life cycles—the dried heads of flowers, grasses that poked through the snow—anything available in a winter landscape. I thought she might appreciate these gifts, understanding things that had been stripped of everything the world called beauty and yet were still startlingly beautiful.

These gifts were kin in my mind to this landscape, which, like the Egyptian desert, was empty in a way that I had never known a landscape to be empty. A tiny strip of a well-worn flag whipped in the wind over our heads and rattled on the flagpole. In one direction, I could see the shimmer of the Dead Sea and, beyond that, the towers of Amman, lit up in the dimming sky.

My husband had arrived, and we'd met up with George, our Palestinian guide, in Bethlehem that morning. George's family had been in Palestine since the Crusades. He had an Italian last name, and his family had made their mark on the region by developing the ubiquitous olivewood carvings sold in every market stall in the Old City. He took us along the family's row of workshops where workers carved camels and donkeys and nativity sets.

George was a gaunt, deeply tanned man with blue eyes and a shaved head. During the hiking season, he worked as a wilderness guide. In the off-season, he went back to the family workshops. He longed to leave Palestine and raise his young children somewhere else, preferably not behind a wall. He and his wife were applying to move to Italy—to return to his ancestral homeland, as he saw it. Meanwhile, he became a wilderness guide, taking tourists like us along a path called the Masar al-Ibrahim, the Abraham Path. This was a route intended to be developed like the Appalachian Trail, guiding people to walk along the ancient route of Abraham, engaging alternative tourists in the history, spirituality, and contemporary realities of the region from a Palestinian point of view.

Mary's path overlapped with Abraham's for a few miles in the Wadi Qelt, and we planned to reach this overlap via a trek through the desert. George had only walked this particular route one other time, from the opposite direction, with a German athlete in February—a significantly cooler month. The question of the heat was a pressing one for us. Hiking season had not really begun. It was still plenty hot, whatever Diana had said about Cross Weather.

The first day, we walked through Bethlehem and its neighbor to the east, Beit Sahour, then along dusty roads out into the desert. I felt like we were walking in a land of eyes, watched but not necessarily welcomed everywhere we went. George was a quiet man, not inclined to small talk, and he didn't translate what the children who followed us out of the last village were calling out to us. Even though he greeted everyone we passed with some form of "Salaam," he didn't address these children. Whatever they were saying, it didn't sound like "Welcome."

We ended the day at a Bedouin camp, made specifically for Abraham Path walkers. It was a collection of small buildings and a tent where we gathered to eat chicken and rice with French hikers.

As I looked out over the landscape that first night, I found it hard to imagine Mary of Egypt's trek across the desert. How could she rush out of Jerusalem on a whim, in September, and make it to the Jordanian wilderness? How would she not get lost or die of thirst? She didn't exactly carry plastic water bottles. Did she ask monks along the way if she was headed in the right direction? Would she, a city girl, have had any idea how to navigate via rocks and stars?

"Does anybody ever not finish these hikes?" my husband had asked George earlier in the day when we were sweating under a fierce sun.

"No," George had said.

2.

My husband is, among other things, a religious skeptic. He is not one to peer into his experience looking for signs, as I had now been doing for weeks. When talk turns to existential questions or supernatural wonders, he usually wanders off looking for something more interesting to do. But if you need someone to walk across the desert with you, I would nominate him. He's got an unrelenting dry sense of humor combined with incessant curiosity. He can always think of a question to ask a stranger. He doesn't take anyone or anything too seriously, and he delights in having strange experiences for their own sake.

Peter and I had both grown up in the American West, and we still lived there. This meant that stories of the Native peoples who had lived on the land before "my" people came were very much a part of our lives. Their names were embedded in place names and their ways of life in how we talked about the landscape. I had known many Indigenous people throughout my life, and the violence of the history of what my people had done to claim the land was not foreign to me. I also knew the ways that Western settlers had erased the stories of Native peoples and replaced them with their own ideologies. Not long before this trip, I'd traveled to my home state of South Dakota and visited an Indian reservation. On one side of the reservation boundary was a water tower painted with the words, "Make America Native Again." Right on the other side, pointed in the direction of the water tower, was a row of Trump campaign signs. Conflict over land and what it means was familiar to me, but here in the Judean Desert, that conflict was both more visible and less visible than I was used to.

There were no campaign signs. There were also no water towers or any visible water. But I knew that the relationship between land and story was perhaps stronger here than anywhere else in the world. Competition for what the land meant and to whom it belonged had been the passionate subject of conversation of nearly everyone we had met while in Israel.

Meanwhile, I was struck by how Mary of Egypt, the quintessential powerless outsider, had no claim on the land through which she traveled. She never would have made it through a checkpoint. She was a landless refugee. Her search for peace, for wholeness, was not a journey to create belonging or to stake a claim anywhere. Mary had not left a mark on the land. She had planted no flags, built no chapels.

As Mary walked through this landscape, her work was to forget her own name, to erase any previous identities. Whatever her name had been when she left the courtyard of the Church of the Holy Sepulchre, that was not her name now. I was now entering the ascetic part of Mary's journey. The ascetic sets out not to withdraw, as it might appear on the surface, but to encounter herself, God, and the created world in a more elemental way.

Some scholars have claimed that the ascetic life is "by its very nature authoritarian" because of its tendency toward extreme personal regulation. But Mary walked in the exact opposite direction—away from any authority but inner authority, away from any regulation but what the landscape and her inner guidance offered. She did what she had to do to become as large as the sky, not to become a point on a landscape. "Mary . . . will not suffer enclosure," scholar Virginia Burrus writes. "She is as vast—and as uncompromisingly elemental in her passions— as the desert itself."

Desire led Mary into this landscape, but it was a different desire than the many she had known previously. It was a desire to create a connection between her own small life and the greater Life. Wherever Mary had been, however unlit the path, God had always been unfolding. That is, to me, one of the key messages of Mary's life: God is everywhere, always unfolding. We can look for signs and wonders because God is always seeking us. When a young girl runs away from home—no matter what she has suffered or why she is running—God is there. If she stands on the seashore, full of desire, God is there. When she turns to face herself, God is there. And when she says, "God was seeking my repentance," I hear, "God was always unfolding, everywhere in everything."

But now the path became bright and clear. She trusted that this crazy rush out into uncertainty would bring her life. It was a wild risk that could easily lead to death. Among the many challenges and uncertainties, she could die of thirst or hunger, the weather or a mountain lion could kill her, and roaming bandits could rape her and leave her for dead. But somehow this risk had become worth taking. It was the only thing to be done.

This is what it means to be on the path of the Wild Woman. You risk becoming nothing more than bones in an empty landscape. But you go in that direction because now the thought of not living the truest possible life is unbearable. The call to life is greater than the fear of death. Whatever Mary's inner guide was choosing for her, she would rather have that than any other reward.

"Don't be a fool," writes Estés. "Go back and stand under that one red flower and walk straight ahead for that last hard mile. Go up and knock on the old weathered door. Climb up to the cave. Crawl through the window of a dream. Sift the desert and see what you find. It is the only work we *have* to do."

3.

Our chance to sift the desert was on the next day, our longest day of hiking. We were hiking from Mar Saba—the monastery where Dan urged me to ask for Father Philaret—to a Bedouin guesthouse on the far side of the desert, a distance of slightly over twelve miles. The sun climbed as we ate a haphazard breakfast with the French tourists of somewhat sandy scrambled eggs and thick yogurt with pita and *fuul*.

The sun climbed still farther as we drove toward Mar Saba and stopped in a nearby town to pick up fresh bread. Well after 9:00 a.m., we finally pulled up to the entrance of the ancient monastery for the beginning of our hike. Even though the morning grew late and was getting later, I felt I couldn't be standing at the entrance and not ask for Father Philaret.

Since I could not go into the monastery, Peter and George got instructions from Brother Ephraim at the front door: "Go inside and call for Father Philaret."

"Call him, like on a telephone? Does he have a number?"

"No. Call out for him."

"Do you know where he is?" Peter asked.

"No, how would I know? I don't know what work he is doing today. Every day is different."

I sat on the stone wall outside while Peter and George bent low through the little door that led to the monastery. It had been built in the fourth century, maybe one hundred years after the Monastery of St. Anthony, when monks from Egypt had made their way to this desert and adapted the ideas of Christian asceticism to it. The front area was crowded with female Greek tourists. The men of the tour group had, I presumed, gone inside. A man with a hatchback had parked in front of the door and served pilgrims coffee with cardamom from a gold-and-red pot.

When Peter and George returned, George raised his eyebrows to me. "He said he would come out in 'awhile.'"

But Father Philaret came out quickly and joined Peter and me on the stone wall. He was Russian, with a little gray in his straggly black beard and bright blue eyes. Dan had told me that he had been an IT executive in Russia before becoming a monk.

He was a little startled and even confused that Dan had told us to ask him for a story about Mary of Egypt.

"I know one story about a woman who came to our monastery," he said. "But it isn't that one." He said there was a nun who lived for a long time in a cave near the monastery, and no one had known she was there. Then one day, a donkey fell into her cave. She was discovered and had to leave.

I felt discouraged by this story and its rendering. What had compelled me in Dan's telling was mutual affection. In that story, the monks had gone after the woman and tried to find her. They sought reconciliation and connection. Here we had, at least on the surface, a story of a woman who needed something, longed for something so much that she "broke the rules" to get it. When she was found out, she was sent away.

End of story. What happened to her? Where did she go? Did she ever find what she needed?

I took a nervous glance at George and asked Father Philaret, "What do you see as the significance of Mary of Egypt for today?"

"An icon of repentance, of course," he answered without pause. "An icon of the all-defeating love of God. Whatever miserable life you have, God is waiting for you. God waits for everybody. You can always repent. With the last breath, you can repent. This is why the story of Mary of Egypt is read in the Great Lent.

"And the other thing is self-rejection. Self-rejection is a crucial part of the Christian way. But it has always been misunderstood from the beginning. When you begin a path of self-rejection, you often think, *This is not what I was talking about. This is too hard.* Then you can look at the life of Mary of Egypt, look at the fruits of her life. The story offers you a chance to see the rewards, if you continue on the path, even though the enemy is always waiting for you and trying to convince you to give up on what you have started."

We said goodbye to Father Philaret and started climbing out of the Kidron Valley, a steep scramble to the top of a long, dry plateau. We looked back at the monastery clinging to a cliff above the foamy water of a polluted creek that dumped sewage from Jerusalem into a once pristine valley.

I had heard many times that Mary was an icon of repentance. As I perceived it, this meant what Father Philaret had said: Even if you are as miserable a human being as Mary of Egypt, God still wants to save you. Surely you are not as bad a sinner as she was! She is the worst possible sinner we could imagine. A woman who liked sex and had a lot of it! Therefore, you can have confidence that God wants to save you too. Sometimes when Mary is lifted up in Orthodox theology as a model for repentance, people talk about the symmetry between the seventeen years she spent in "sin" as a prostitute in Alexandria and the seventeen years of atonement that she practiced in the desert before being released into a greater peace. This version of atonement—an eye for an eye—didn't speak to me.

As a woman, I was sensitive to the potential for self-loathing lurking here. Father Philaret had used a slightly different term—*self-rejection*—and there were key differences, but these could be easily overlooked and mis-understood, especially in a tradition with the capacity to be as misogy-nistic as Christianity. I knew how close self-loathing could live in the Christian tradition to kenosis—the radical outpouring of oneself for the sake of love. I knew the damage it could do. If self-loathing com-pelled me to follow in the footsteps of Mary of Egypt, I could just as well have stayed at home. I had plenty of that where I came from.

If this was not a path of all-encompassing love, then it was an awful lot of work for nothing. While repentance, in Father Philaret's version, emphasized the radical break in Mary's life, I was just as curious about the continuities. As I meditated on her story, I wondered about the way that her desire for others led her to desire the ultimate Other, God. I was fascinated that she pursued her new desire with the same wild passion and energy with which she had pursued the previous ones. In fact, when she told Zosimas the story of her life, she ended by telling him that she had an "unrestrained desire" for the "life-giving gifts" of the Eucharist. While the object of her desire was now radically dif-ferent, the force of her desire had the same might. Desire itself, for all its disparagement in the Christian tradition, had been her deepest motivation.

As we began our hike across the long desert plateau under the nearly midday sun, I thought about the pieces of the story that I knew had claimed me. For example, there was the moment when Zosimas brought Mary a basket of figs and soaked lentils, and she took these precious gifts, offered in love and admiration, to her lips. I thought of the way that he wrapped a cloak around her shoulders. The way he listened to her story with an almost desperate need to understand. "God wills our freedom," writes Sara Maitland, a modern solitary and sometime desert dweller and author of *A Book of Silence*. "Because of that, God is very unlikely to bully you."

4.

Zosimas—Mary's last lover—might have set out from a monastery like Mar Saba across this very plain as I was doing. The text says that he was from one of the "old monasteries." Mar Saba was one of them, and on this trek, we would encounter two others. One was another cliff monastery, the Monastery of St. George in the Wadi Qelt, and the other was on the Jericho plain closer to the place where Mary crossed the river, the Monastery of St. Gerasimos.

The story of Zosimas's search for Mary began in a place like Mar Saba, where monks strove to be the greatest spiritual athletes, to overcome every desire and every impulse in order to clamber up a ladder toward God. Zosimas was good at being a monk in this way: "He pursued every outward form of asceticism. He accustomed himself to every kind of self-discipline and followed every rule that had been handed down by those who knew and had trained in this arena of spiritual struggle. He also kept many rules that he himself thought up as he sought to subordinate the flesh to the spirit. And in this goal, he did not miss the mark. This monk was a symbol of spirituality, and many often came from monasteries near and far to be molded and trained in self-discipline by his teaching."

But one day, when he was fifty-three years old, he said to himself, "Where is there a monk in the world who has surpassed me? Who has proven greater than me in practice?" Zosimas recognized with both sadness and pride that he had no teachers left.

Then another mysterious voice intervened. The text does not tell us how Zosimas received the profound insight that changed the course of his life and now had changed the course of mine. It merely says that "someone came near" to Zosimas. Was this a real person? An interior voice? An angel? A divine voice? There is no clue in the manuscript. But a teacher—whether internal or external—was found just when Zosimas realized he had no teachers. This "someone" said to him, "Greater is the struggle before you than the one that has passed. . . . In order that you may learn how many roads there are to salvation, go from the land of your kindred and from the house of your father . . . Go to the monastery that is near the river Jordan."

This intimate voice told Zosimas that the spiritual struggle is long and hard and there is no place in it for self-satisfaction. He had yet to learn "how many roads there are to salvation." He must go out into the unknown, away from his judgments and into uncertainty. I thought of something that Peter said as we hiked up out of the Kidron Valley. He knew that I was usually in thrall to monks and ascetics, to anyone who chose these solitary paths. But now after listening to Father Philaret, he said, "You know what bugs me about monks? It's the self-certainty." This was a tendency in Christian monasticism that I had often overlooked. It was the one Zosimas had left home to escape.

As we hiked across the barren desert for the next six hours under an unrelenting sun, I was struck by Zosimas's courage. Many times I thought of the green Nile valley, of Mido, and of refreshing ginger drinks. I fantasized about taking Peter there and resting with him in the shade of ancient cassia trees or floating along the river. What fool's errand had I taken my husband on? No doubt, he had drawn the short end of the stick.

5.

"Last shade of the day," George called out. We drank some water under the shelter of a rock.

"This hike might just be stupid," Peter muttered to me. It was 12:30. "I don't know if I would recommend it to anyone."

We climbed to a high point where we could see Jerusalem in one direction and the sparkle of the Dead Sea in another.

After another hour, Peter said, "Have you noticed that George isn't drinking as much water as we are?"

"Maybe he is more used to the heat," I said. "Maybe he doesn't need as much."

But as the afternoon wore on, George began to slow. He stopped more frequently. At first it was just to point out a few landscape features—a collared dove, a black start, a lizard, a snakeskin left under a rock. But eventually he stopped just to stop.

Peter and I began to hike ahead of him. We were restless to get to our destination, to get out of the sun, and we seemed to be holding up a little better than George. I offered him one of the oral hydration tablets that had been like fuel to me.

"I don't have any water left," he said. I looked down at my own water bottle. I had only about half a liter. I held it out to him. He refused.

I looked into George's gaunt face, which looked even thinner as he gasped against a rock without water and without shade. His cheeks were sunken, like he had become all skull.

"It's OK," he said. "I called for a donkey."

I laughed, then I realized that George was not joking.

"Keep going," he said. "It's not far."

Peter and I kept walking, leaving George behind us. *It's not far*, George had said. He had not said that the next section of the hike was the most treacherous. The two-foot-wide path dropped off into a yellow-rocked gorge. The path sloped slightly toward it. One wrong move and you could slide into the gorge with nothing to stop you. We walked with concentration. Every once in a while, Peter would ask, "You OK?"

I had no answer except "Yes." The truth was, I couldn't, in that moment, discern OK from not OK. I only knew that each step had to be made until we reached the end of the precipice. There was no other way.

Just as we reached the end of the gorge, we saw two boys on donkeys coming toward us. They looked precarious on the narrow path, but they rode on, expressionless. One boy passed us toward George as we pressed ourselves up against the rock on the nongorge side of the path. The other boy stopped in front of us and then turned around without speaking, as if to lead us into the valley.

Now that we were off the ledge, Peter began hiking a good distance in front of me, and the boy on the donkey arranged himself just behind Peter to herd him (so it seemed to me) toward the camp. I saw a spray of black goats on the hill and white tents below that. As the sky turned lavender, I saw Peter disappear into the camp. Behind me, I heard George and the other donkey.

I descended past the goats. An old man rested on a cot under a pavilion. "*Salaam aleiykum*," I said.

"*Aleiykum salaam*," he said and pointed me toward the guest tent.

Finally—cool water and a place to sit out of the sun. I felt like I had been boiled or set on fire. The embers of that fire were still below the surface of my skin. Everything hurt.

The camp was rustic. It had not been created for tourists like the last one. We were staying in someone's home. The small building where we put our bags looked like a storage container turned into a schoolroom. There were small tables where children were working, playing, and running in and out. The children looked at us like we were not quite human, like they understood on an intellectual level that we were of the same species, but they didn't quite buy it. When I smiled, they did not change their expressions.

We sat down on the long couches of the guest tent. George had at last arrived on the donkey and was drinking Coca-Cola and smoking a cigarette. I was relieved to see him. Boys brought out a parade of dishes from the kitchen: rice and chicken, tomatoes and cucumbers, hummus, and chewy Bedouin bread.

That night, I lay on a mat in the schoolroom listening to dogs bark and mice scratch. The donkeys gave off wild calls. As I tried to fall asleep, I felt that precipice's edge, the sensation of having nothing between me and the deep yellow gorge. My mind and stomach lurched as though I were about to fall.

When at last I slept for a few minutes between the dogs barking, I dreamed the word *besoin*—the French word for "need"—which rose up from my subconscious from some high school French class. But in my dream, the word meant both "drink" and "without."

6.

The next morning, a car took us to a spot above the Wadi Qelt where we were to meet up with the route of Mary of Egypt.

The Wadi Qelt is a canyon that runs directly from Jerusalem to Jericho along an ancient Roman aqueduct. Geographically speaking, it runs along the Aegean Sea Plate across the dry Eurasian Steppe and onto the Great Rift Valley. This means that even as Mary walked the fifteen-mile distance, she traipsed continents as if she had grown cosmically long legs.

The first thing we noticed about the Wadi Qelt was water. We stopped at a spring, where we soaked our aching bodies and swam with tiny fish that nibbled our toes. George—somewhat recovered from the previous day's exertions—said this was actually the third spring in the Wadi Qelt between here and Jerusalem. Suddenly Mary's rushed exit from Jerusalem and arrival in Jericho on the same day made sense. She followed an established route and had plenty of water to drink along the way. While Zosimas might have crossed the deathly desert that we had just traversed, she had likely not.

The landscape, thanks to water, had changed dramatically. Green plants poured off the canyon walls. We heard birds calling and followed the aqueduct onto the steep canyon rim. We hiked to the Monastery of

St. George, which like Mar Saba was built into the cliff wall. There we drank the lemonade the monks provided to tourists.

"What is the relationship of this monastery to Mary of Egypt?" George asked one of the monks.

"She passed this way," he said matter-of-factly.

I wondered if she had seen monks on the cave-pocked landscape in their black hoods. I wondered if she walked on their bridges and paths leading from isolated cell to isolated cell. I imagined that they stared at the ground as she passed and that she passed them quickly—her errand too great for much stopping.

I knew that Andrew of Crete had also composed his Triodion to Mary from this monastery—a liturgy in the Orthodox Church that is the reason that Mary of Egypt is remembered by so many. In one of the rooms of the monastery, there was an icon of Mary and Zosimas. In this icon, the young woman kneeling before the Virgin Mary that I had seen at the Church of the Holy Sepulchre is replaced by an old woman stooped before Zosimas, bending to receive the Eucharist from a small spoon that he is holding.

I wondered why this was the moment from Mary's story that the monastery had chosen to immortalize. I supposed that it reinforced Father Philaret's version of Mary as an icon of repentance. Mary becomes all of us, bending before the priest, asking for what we cannot receive on our own. But there were other moments that could have been equally meaningful. When Zosimas and Mary first meet, for example, they argue about who is going to bow to whom. The text says that they both lay on the ground before the other "for an interval of many hours" while they each asked the other for a blessing. Zosimas won that argument, and Mary blessed him. There was the moment when Mary walked on water across the Jordan to meet Zosimas on the other side. Or the moment when the lion licked dead Mary's feet.

Many moments might have hinted at the complexity in this story: the combination of wild longing and deep connection. The choice to render

Mary's reception of the Eucharist as the central scene in their encounter erased the fact that Zosimas was the one doing the learning. It elevated the institution over the desert, Zosimas over Mary, the domesticated over the wild. Is this how Mary was remembered in the desert? I was as close to her path as I had yet been, but somehow I felt she was missing.

MELT

1.

We arrived at the date palm–strewn Jericho plain where the Wadi Qelt ends at a ruin of Herod's winter palace. The ruin smelled of goat piss and garbage. The air was hot and heavy.

A taxi took us to the Mudhouse Guesthouse, organized by a women's collective at the Aqbat Jaber Refugee Camp. Both Peter and I were somewhat desperately hoping it would have showers and be rodent- and barking dog–free. A woman named Umm Fares (mother of Fares) greeted us and showed us a small, simple room where we would sleep. She had a long face, brown eyes, and a black robe with a few sequins on it. A black underscarf hid her hair with a brown hijab over it.

I was immediately drawn to her. Her eyes sparkled with understanding, and her every gesture was impeccably kind. When she spoke, I felt I understood her. She likewise thought that I spoke Arabic, and for the first time, I understood phrases and words that had been opaque for weeks. When George said, "She thinks you speak Arabic," I laughed. "I only speak Umm Fares," I said.

She brought us a huge plate of rice with chickpeas and baked chicken, Arab salad, and tea with mint. We showered and climbed gratefully into clean single beds. In the morning, she greeted us again with *shakshuka*—eggs in a rich tomato sauce—and bread dipped in olive oil and za'atar, a thyme-sesame seasoning. Through each meal and kindness, Umm Fares offered us what I had longed to offer Mary all those years ago under the New Mexican moon: a homecoming, a welcome back to ourselves after the relentless strain of the desert.

2.

Now in Jericho, we had two sites on my map to visit. One was the baptismal site—this is the place where Jesus was baptized by John. In Mary's day, there was a monastery here, perhaps one oriented to pilgrims. She took communion at this monastery and spent the night. She tells Zosimas, "As the sun was setting, I reached the Church of John the Baptist situated near the Jordan. Before going down to the Jordan, I first worshipped in the church. Then I immediately washed my face and hands with that holy water. I partook of the undefiled and life-giving sacrament at the Church of the Forerunner, and ate half a loaf of bread and drank from the Jordan. Then I laid myself down on the earth for the night."

The church where she stopped is long gone. These days, on the Israeli side, this site is largely unexcavated and undeveloped. Many Christian tourists come here to dip themselves in the muddy river in baptismal gowns that you can buy for $12. But the remains of the old monasteries are still buried under the remnants of the war between Israel and Jordan that officially ended in 1994.

As we drove toward the baptismal site, George pointed out the cameras everywhere. On either side of us were a military fence and an eerie no-man's land. When we reached a checkpoint, our driver said to the soldiers, "I've got Americans," and we were waved through without even a checking of documents. George said that even when he has Europeans in his van, the driver says, "I've got Americans" because that works like a password—like "Open Sesame."

Everywhere in our hike through Palestine, we felt and heard signs of unrest and of war. This day in Jericho, the city was on strike because a Bedouin camp, perhaps not unlike the one where we had spent our night in the desert, was being threatened by Israeli bulldozers, the occupants told they had to move so their village could be destroyed. Across the desert, George had frequently bent down to show us bullets and shell casings. He had shown us how the trail markers that he helped set up along the way were taken down and replaced with Israeli markers. It frequently struck George afresh how strange and unfair it was that he and his family had ended up on this side of the wall with the cameras and guns and bulldozers pointed at them.

The baptismal site itself was a heavily guarded swamp. Israeli soldiers with AK-47s stood on one side of the thick river while Jordanian guards stood, similarly armed, on the other side, a distance of no more than twenty-five yards. We could have waded from one side to the other in less than a minute. In Mary's day, the Jordan River was much wider, but now a lot of the water has been drained off by the Israelis to irrigate the Negev Desert. According to George, when the peace accords with Jordan were signed, Israeli was granted 60 percent of the Jordan's water, Jordan was granted 40 percent, and the Palestinians got 0 percent. It was a three-way deal.

Besides signs of the conflict, there was not much to see here. I tried to imagine the water of the Jordan filling the whole space on which we and every other tourist on both sides of the river stood. I tried to imagine Mary needing a boat to get from one side to the other. What stayed with me was the vision of two sets of soldiers with two sets of machine guns across a tiny, muddy stream.

3.

We stopped next at the Monastery of St. Gerasimos of the Jordan. Like Mar Saba and St. George, St. Gerasimos was one of the "old monasteries," but instead of being a cliff monastery, it had been built on the Jericho plain, near the Jordan. It had been built on this spot in the fifth century by a monk who had come to Palestine from Turkey. Now the grounds had been converted into a park where West Bank families came to picnic. Peacocks and roosters roamed the fruit tree–covered landscape.

I imagined that, as with the Monastery of St. George, there would be some indication that Mary of Egypt had "passed this way." But along the way, The Quest had yielded only small glimpses of her, hard-won signs of the story I was tracing. So I was surprised by the sudden embarrassment of riches inside St. Gerasimos. Everywhere I looked, there was an image of Mary of Egypt. Several images were being sold at the gift shop. In the narthex, where a nun with swollen ankles and thick socks in Birkenstocks grunted at us as a greeting, there was an image of Mary. Inside the church, she dominated an entire corner.

On one wall of that corner, there was a badly damaged fresco of Mary of Egypt and Zosimas standing side by side, of the same height, and even the same age. She had her hands folded across her heart. He looked like he was holding something—a staff, maybe. Her hair was wild on her head and her robe shabby, reminiscent of icons of John the Baptist. They looked intent, like two people from an old photograph. There was power in both of them, a kind of equally balanced power, like no other representation or icon I had yet seen.

On the iconostasis, there were multiple images of Mary and Zosimas, all of them variations on Mary receiving communion, like the one I had seen at St. George in the Wadi Qelt. I sat for a long time in a pew in that corner, surrounded at last by the memory of the person I had sought.

The mountains of Jordan in the icons, the river, the dry wilderness around her—all were now familiar to me. It was where I had been, where I was now, and where I was going.

While I sat, trying to take this in, Peter and George had grown bored and gone outside to sit under the fruit trees. In the hot silence after they left, I was surprised again by my tears. I hadn't cried since we left Jerusalem, probably because my body didn't have extra water to spare. But now between the tears and the sweat, the sense I'd had at the Cave of St. Anthony—that I was becoming liquid—intensified. I imagined melting and becoming a part of the Jordan. Last seen, they would say, on the banks of the Jordan River, having dissolved.

The whole road behind me—all of the miles of The Quest—felt like it could end here, with a few icons in a church. I had told the story of Mary of Egypt to countless people and had seen no recognition in their eyes. Just downstairs at the table where a monk sold postcards, when I had asked about a postcard of Mary of Egypt, he had shoved one toward me with no hint of care. I had confessed over and over to myself and to others that I didn't know what I was chasing, and here the reality of that set in in a new way. Maybe it had all come to nothing.

I thought of the nun outside, who had now taken off her sandals and put her swollen feet up on the bench and fallen asleep. Did she feel bitter about her choice to give everything to the religious life? Was that what made her so grumpy? You work so hard, you follow the signs the best you are able, you are obedient to the call you think is in you, and you end up sitting for hours in a hot room attending to tourists.

I looked over at the fresco of Mary staring down at me with intensity in her eyes. My friend Marge, a woman of almost ninety, had half-affectionately, half-teasingly said before I left that I was going to the Middle East to "feel the atmosphere." A lot of miles, a massive carbon footprint, a lot of time away from my family to walk a legend and find a couple of icons in the corner of a church.

As I felt this sense of ending, all the endings came crashing in on me. What if my own St. George Church in Leadville was going to die? What if Ali was going to die? There was nothing I could do about it. All the life-giving mysteries, as Mary might call them, that I had known to this point were passing away.

Eventually the tears subsided. I hadn't dissolved. I tiptoed past the sleeping nun. Peter and George sat out in the shade.

"I told Peter," George said with a wink, "maybe Amy isn't coming back. Maybe she's decided to stay here and become a nun."

I thought about the fresco, still feeling the gaze of Mary on me—that gathered power. I thought of the moment in the text when Zosimas bent down at Mary's feet and grasped them but then let go because he "could not hold for long the one who would not be held." To accept that, to accept the lightest touch on that which could not be held, this was perhaps one of the hardest moments in the desert's teachings. I had walked a long way to practice letting go.

BE WILD

1.

The day after my meltdown at the Monastery of St. Gerasimos, we crossed into Jordan. Our journey was much more convoluted than Mary's. Mary woke up on the west side of the Jordan River and then "found a small boat" on the riverbank. She used it to cross over the river and then asked her inner guide where to go. "From that time until now," she told Zosimas, "I have lived far off in exile and in this wilderness I have made my home, waiting for my God, the one who protects those who turn toward him from faintheartedness and hard winds."

We, on the other hand, took two taxis and a bus to cross a distance of less than a mile. We stood in line for more than an hour to process paperwork and pay fees. When we finally stumbled out on the Jordanian side, I hoped we had done all that was required to be here legitimately, but I wasn't entirely sure.

I had low expectations for our time in Jordan, insofar as The Quest was concerned. I didn't have a specific destination in mind. The manuscript that served as my map did not help us. For the east side of the Jordan, it said things like "the deeper desert" and "the heart of the desert." These were not things that you could look up or ask a guide to take you to. The Jordan River itself seemed to be the last remaining geographical marker that could be found on an actual map. Once we had crossed it, I didn't know what we should do.

Before leaving the United States, I'd contacted a small company on the advice of a friend. I told the American owner, who worked in partnership with Jordanians to run an ecotourism outfit, the story of Mary of Egypt and I asked where he'd recommend we go to find what the desert tradition calls the *via avia*, the way of no way.

It might have been the oddest request he'd received, but he handled it as if he'd taken the question a hundred times before.

"The landscape of Jordan," he said, "has changed a lot in fifteen hundred years. It's a volatile place; earthquakes, floods, droughts, political and military battles have all shaped and reshaped the landscape." But just as I considered dropping the Jordan part of our trip altogether, he added, "If you want to see the ancient landscape of Jordan, I would recommend a place called Wadi al Hasa."

"OK," I said. I didn't have an alternative. "Take us there."

A young man named Jawad met us and helped us complete still more paperwork before we loaded into a van. In the van, Jawad told us he had been an accountant but hated desk work so much that he had become a wilderness guide.

"Every day I am not at a desk is a good day," he said.

His task was to take us to the baptismal site, where we had been the day before on the Israeli side. Then we would spend the night at the Dead Sea, and in the morning, we would go to Wadi al Hasa with another guide.

Jawad assured us that there was much more to see on the Jordanian side of the baptismal site. This was because, after the 1994 peace accord with Israel, a Jordanian archaeologist named Mohamed Waheeb had been eager to excavate the site he believed held the greatest riches of both Judaism and Christianity. He and his team had received permission to begin excavation and hadn't stopped since. Jordan had also opened up the site to Christians who wanted to build small chapels. The place buzzed with activity.

"I see from your itinerary that you are religious," Jawad said.

I glanced at Peter. I knew this wasn't a word he would have used. Was The Quest religious? I hadn't actually asked this question.

"I myself am not religious," Jawad went on, sparing us the difficulty of explaining. "I am Muslim. My family is Muslim. But I am not practicing." At the beginning, Jawad said, his mother worried for him. "I pray for you," she told him. "I pray you find God. I pray for your safety. I pray for your soul."

I asked why Jawad could not go through the motions to make his mother happy.

"There's a Muslim concept," he said, "called *khushour*. It means 'spiritual presence.' You cannot just go through the motions. You've got to show up for your prayers with *khushour*. That's what I cannot do."

Jawad took us to a small Greek Orthodox Church near the water. The construction was new, and the icons inside were new as well. There was the smell of fresh paint. Here there were more icons of Mary of Egypt, as at the Monastery of St. Gerasimos, in prominent locations. They were again the images of a bent Mary bowing to receive communion from a priestly Zosimas. I felt the same inner sigh. This was not what I was looking for. Mary mattered here, but only in a particular way that missed the wild beauty I had found in her story, a beauty wild enough to compel me out of my complacency in search of my own version of *khushour*. Whatever it was that I was looking for—the door, the key, the answer to my question, the so what, the direction, the way—it was not here. *Maybe the* khushour *is missing in me*, I thought. *Maybe I just don't get it.*

Jawad had stayed by the door while Peter and I walked around the chapel. He was talking to the Muslim doorkeeper, and when we returned, no doubt my disappointment was written on my face.

"Guys," Jawad said. "You know what? The guard says that there is a site dedicated to Mary of Egypt just down the path here."

A site dedicated to Mary of Egypt? What did that even mean? Was it a plaque or a cave or a chapel? Why was it there? As we hurried down the dusty but well-marked path, I tried to imagine what we might be preparing to see. I reached into the recesses of my brain, trying to remember if I had ever read anything about this anywhere. In my fifteen years of research, in the stacks of books I had ordered from the library, from any of my guides—Dan or the many Orthodox people I had spoken to—had any of them ever mentioned a site of Mary of Egypt? Had there been a stray footnote that I had missed? Nothing. Nowhere. Never.

Farther down the path, we saw the ruins of two Byzantine-era buildings. They were, according to the sign, pilgrimage houses built in the fifth or sixth century and added on to during the Ottoman period. After being destroyed by earthquake and flood, they were rebuilt by local people in the nineteenth century and destroyed again during the Israeli-Jordan war.

They had been built, the archaeologist believed, for pilgrims following in the footsteps of Mary of Egypt. There were so many pilgrims, and they had come so consistently for so long, that houses had to be built for them. The sign said that local tradition called these houses the "palace of the lady." This instantly struck me as a kind of ironic joke: these were not palaces. But at the same time, the phrase contained affection and homage in the midst of irony. The lady—people had come here to follow her, to make contact with her mystery, to see what she had seen. A thousand years later, they still spoke of her with honor.

Here in front of my eyes was an entire pilgrimage tradition for the one who could not be followed, for the "one who would not be held."

The site was empty of visitors except for the three of us. I bent down and touched the stones that were gray and white, covered with a fine dust—limestone, I guessed from my reading. I had expected nothing, and not exactly in the Buddhist sense of expecting nothing, as the lama had advised Peter Matthiessen. No, I had actually expected nothing because I had no idea there might be something. In that place was an entire lost tradition.

Mary was remembered here not by American scholars and not even by monks, as far as I could tell, but by ordinary people who knew this place and remembered its story and by a Muslim archaeologist who had believed something might be found here. I felt surrounded by a cloud of witnesses. People had come to this place looking for her—perhaps even during her lifetime, maybe only shortly after—and they had continued to come for hundreds of years. Right here, to this place that my hands now touched, her pilgrims had come.

As I felt the stone under my fingers, I felt the story changing. I was not alone. I had never been alone. I was just a thousand years late. Numerous others had felt the wild mystery and been drawn toward it.

Later I read the monograph that Mohamed Waheeb had prepared about his discovery of the site. I had to order it from Jordan; it wasn't available in the United States. In *The Discovery of Site of St. Mary of Egypt*, Dr. Waheeb discusses how the place, at first, did not seem ancient enough for the archaeological team's attention and how it was strewn with the remnants left by Jordanian soldiers. He writes that the site was "surrounded by tamarisk trees from all sides" and "bordered by the Lissan marl cliffs with its caves to the east, by the Jordan River to the west, and by the famous remains of John the Baptist church 100m to the south." But as they uncovered the remains of the buildings, they began to connect what they were seeing with the writing of a French archaeologist working in the area in the 1930s and then with the testimony of local people. All of that led them to Mary of Egypt.

I looked up toward the "Lissan marl" cliffs and saw steps leading up to a cave. The rock of the cave, when we climbed up to it, was clean and freshly swept as if a monk had just come and gone.

The tradition that I followed was still alive, if hidden. Here it was tangible, lived, immediate, present—Mary, the monks, Zosimas, pilgrims, me. Along the way, Mary had been like the snow leopard—elusive, a tease. Now I was on her ground, in her place. Standing in front of these halls, touching these rocks, I stood in a long, continuous tradition begun by a nameless, homeless, unknown woman, Mary of Egypt. I could feel that she was remembered, cared for, spoken of, followed.

For the first time, I was bewildered in exactly the way the spiritual journey promised. I felt the wildness, the impossibility of it all, blowing through me like a wind across the desert.

2.

This was difficult to take in. Heading away from the baptismal site in a state of wonder, I couldn't quite adjust to the Dead Sea hotel, the flood of tourists, the monstrous buffet. It did not resonate. I kept returning to my wonder, quietly inside myself, and turning it over and over. I didn't suppose that Jawad could quickly secure permission for me to sleep in one of the caves above her site. I didn't ask.

The next morning, a van pulled up in front of our hotel to take us to Wadi al Hasa. Our new guide was a man named Monther—dreadlocked, playful, with a long beard and a mischievous smile.

"I am excited to take you to a magical place called Wadi al Hasa," Monther said as the driver pulled out of the parking lot and began driving south along the Dead Sea.

"Wait!" I wanted to say. "I think we are going the wrong way." Having now touched the rocks at Mary of Egypt's "palace," I had imagined us hiking not far from there. I didn't want to go to another wilderness. I wanted to stay close to the traces I had found. Maybe I had made a mistake with the owner of Experience Jordan. Maybe he had not understood me. I felt some dismay as we drove farther and farther south past shantytowns, potash extraction plants, and boys walking to school along the highway.

The story of Mary of Egypt is full of the heat of passion and the motion of travel. Throughout it, people are running, hastening, sweating, and crying hot tears. This is how the "fire of faith" gets lit. Mary of Egypt had somehow also set me in motion. She had propelled me across the world to sweat more than I had sweated in decades, to feel the heat of the desert and to let it set fire in me. Now we were going the wrong way—even if we were rushing off as Mary had. The momentum was greater than the tender, open place of my new discovery. We had no choice but to keep going.

I thought of the way that my mother and I had entered the journey as two human beings and how she had helped me become fierce in The Quest, like one of St. Anthony's lions, and how Peter had helped me plod forward through the desert, one foot after another, oxen-like in our sense of completing the mission, whatever it might bring us. But was there still an eagle out there waiting for me? Was there one more stage of transformation or was this all?

After an hour, we turned up into the Jordanian mountains and continued climbing. We stopped the van on a ridge where a pickup truck was waiting for us. A small man in a checkered kaffiyeh got out and, with a big grin, loaded our bags into the back of his truck. As we piled into the cab of his pickup and Monther tucked himself in with our bags in the back, Abu Ayman talked to us continuously in Arabic as if we might understand him. If we failed to answer something he considered important, he rolled down his window and shouted his question to Monther. Otherwise, he continued to talk to us, as if understanding might suddenly descend on us, like the angel to Mohamed—peace be upon him—and help him out.

Abu Ayman left us at the top of a steep descent. We started down into what Monther told us was an ancient seabed, rich with fossilized coral reef, and the border between two biblical kingdoms—Edom and Moab.

At the bottom of the descent, we found ourselves in a steep ravine with cliffs on either side and a stream running through it.

It became clear quickly that we were going to hike in the stream. In Colorado, we go to pretty big lengths to avoid this. With the cold water and sharp rocks and the fact that you don't want your feet to be wet in an unpredictable environment, hiking in a stream had never been an option. But here in Wadi al Hasa, we waded right in, shoes and all.

"Survival in the Jordanian wilderness 101," Monther said. "Look for the oleander. Oleander needs clean water to grow, so if you see it grow-ing, you know there is good, fresh water, probably a spring nearby." Then he showed us how to walk across a stream. "Don't look down at the water when you are crossing," he said. "Look ahead, where you are going."

Our pace was smooth and natural, the result of walking through water. At the same time, rocks, currents, and the constant changing of the shoreline meant that our attention was required for every step. As we practiced, it became a soft, meditative attention, not a hard, concentrated one. After a few hours, Monther stopped along the shore and boiled water for tea with sage leaves in it. He smoked a cigarette and tucked the butt into the laces of his shoes.

When we started walking again, Monther began to talk about his "real job." He was a guide for an organization called Mercy Corps that takes traumatized Syrian youth out into the wilderness for therapy.

"All I do is show them a few things, give them a little equipment—here's a rope, here's how you tie it—and I let nature do the rest," he declared. "Nature heals them."

He told us about a Yale University study done with the kids he took out in the wilderness. They tested the cortisol/dopamine balance in their saliva before their work with Mercy Corps and then a year after they began. There was a significant change. Cortisol decreased. Dopamine increased. But Monther didn't feel he needed the study to prove this. He could see and feel it. The kids were changing, and nature was changing them. The work was intense, he said, and he often felt that after a week with the kids, he needed to himself go into nature for healing. This coming Saturday, he was heading out on a silent hike from Petra to Wadi Rum to clear his mind and his heart.

He was at home in the wadi. He walked in such peace that it was hard not to feel peaceful too as I followed his footsteps through the stream. With his kaffiyeh, dreadlocks, and scraggly beard, he looked like the American stereotype of an ISIS fighter—except for his exuberant warmth. He told us a story that began with "I used to have a much longer beard." One day, he had attempted a solo hike on part of the Jordan Trail where he hadn't been before. He had mapped out his water sources, but spring after spring was dry. He started to get desperate. At last he saw a truck with local guides and tourists in it, and he knew they would have water. He started toward them at a run. The local guides panicked. One of them pulled out a knife, and the other picked up rocks to throw at him. It took some time to communicate that he was not a terrorist but a water-desperate hiker. "I took from this not 'carry more water' but 'don't grow so long a beard.'" He laughed.

As we walked, I started to do the math. Before this trip, I would have thought that "doing the math" on a fairy tale was a foolish thing to do. But now that I had seen the "site of Mary of Egypt," I thought differently. I had been dismayed about turning away from what I thought was the path of Mary of Egypt. I had imagined a different wilderness. But the *Life of Mary of Egypt* says that Zosimas walked for twenty days to reach the "heart of the wilderness." It was a place with steep canyons and ravines, like the ones that stood around me now—perhaps not quite as steep as these, given sixteen hundred years of water flowing. If Zosimas had walked ten miles a day for twenty days, that is a distance of two hundred miles—almost exactly the distance between the baptismal site and where we now walked. Here Mary would have had water and wild plants. Life in this place could sustain itself.

"Twee-o-weet," I heard a bird call out as if confirming my thoughts.

"Did you hear that bird?" Monther asked. "That's the Tristram's starling. It's my favorite bird. The year I lived in Romania and was homesick, I found YouTube videos with the sound of that bird, and I listened to them over and over."

If this was the place of Mary of Egypt, what would that mean? I thought of the Syrian children that Monther brought here in search of healing, the way that the place itself brought them what was required to begin to transform the broken into something new. What if this was the same "cure" that took Mary of Egypt out into the wilderness? She sought healing in the wild, letting God, in the form of nature, do the work. She sought "bewilderment." In the wilderness, God offered her a few skills and a very small amount of equipment, but the space was large enough that it could hear her whole story—pain and desire, fault and injury, need and seeking. She could find and become the Wild Woman. She became so at one with nature, as the first monks had longed for, that even the elements began to be at her service. She walked on water. She rose into the air. Maybe the lions took refuge with her. The text says that she saw not a single wild creature while she was in the desert, but maybe that is because to her, none of them was wild anymore. Maybe the plants told her their names even as the psalms taught themselves to her.

Maybe this was atonement—that goal of the Christian life, the goal so many had told me was the point of the life of Mary of Egypt. Atonement, "at-one-ment" in its most literal sense, is the bringing together of disparate parts into a unity, a whole. As Mary befriended the wildness in the world and in herself, she drew close to the heart of the wilderness, the essence of the world as it is. She reconciled, atoned, was salved as well as saved.

"What is the way of Mary of Egypt?" Dan had asked. "What was the meaning of Mary of Egypt for today?"

He had been right: you couldn't know the answer to this question without following in her footsteps, without coming to the place where her own reconciliation had occurred. David Jasper had said that Mary of Egypt could not be followed, but as far as I know, he had not tried. He not seen oleander pouring over cliff walls to signal pure water or heard the Tristram's starling call out a confirmation.

She could be followed. Many, many had followed her. Her way was hard—you found it footsore, sweaty, and on the verge of the physically impossible. At the edge of yourself, you stumble onto her. She is already ahead of you in the wilderness—the Wild Woman, that deep woman of myth, who goes away from outer authority to find an inner authority, who goes out into the wilderness to seek bewilderment. We search for, as Estés puts it, "a clue, a remnant, a sign that she still lives, that we have not lost our chance" to find her.

This is what had compelled Zosimas's tears as he ran toward her, having found a sign of her at last. As he ran, he forgot "his old age and the exhaustion of his journey." And when it seemed like she would outrun him on the rocky terrain, he cried out, "Wait for me!" And then he added, as if broken by the possibility that all his searching would come to nothing, "God does not ever detest anyone."

His passion for Mary was his passion for meeting self-transformation. He had risked a great deal, put the old life behind him—a comfortable self, a record of achievement—for the unknown and the unknowable, for an uncharted journey. And what a surprise to meet her here. He had not expected that in a woman, he would meet the wildest and most whole version of himself.

But what exactly is atonement? Is that what the Syrian children had found with Monther as their brains healed? My trek with George and Peter had confirmed that the wilderness is utterly indifferent to any one human's survival. It can break your body as well as your spirit. It can be as quick to destroy as to heal. Desert naturalist Craig Childs has written that in desert landscapes, either you die from thirst or you die from drowning—or, as was nearly the case for me, from slipping off a cliff down into a canyon. And the wildernesses of our lives are not only physical but also metaphorical. Ali had now wandered into the wilderness of cancer, where all of her footsteps felt like precarious ones. Her own body had become that dangerous and desolate land. The cancer was as indifferent as the landscape but more intimate.

As I tried to wade through the current and over the streambed's rocks, I realized that atonement wasn't a healing of the physical body—there was nothing to be guaranteed there. How many times did Mary want to lie down and die? But atonement was walking into the essence of things, touching the stones with your hands, wading through the current in search of what would hold you.

The past, Mary tells Zosimas, will not hold you. It will only torment you with its regrets and its old desires. The future is not secure. What held her in the wilderness was the experience of "a light shining everywhere around me. And then a certain steady calmness came like a huge wave over me."

Wading in the stream for miles made me feel like I didn't even have feet. I lost track of time. I followed my guides—Peter and Monther—ahead of me on the path, paying attention only to the next turn in the streambed and the sandstone canyon with dark streaks on it that looked like words written in a mysterious language.

3.

That night, we pulled up along the stream at a place that Monther jokingly called "the apartment" because it sat on a wide, flat section where we could put tents and had sandstone-hewn "windows" that looked out onto the stream.

He built a fire in a ring of stones using dead palm and some wood that previous campers here had collected as well as branches from a tree he called the "Sodom apple." If someone breaks a bone in the wilderness, he said, you could use this tree to create a splint. He cooked us dinner and set a small circle of votive candles around us. We had descended to 350 meters below sea level, he said. "Let's celebrate!" He brought out a bottle of Jordanian Cabernet Sauvignon from his backpack and poured us mugs of it.

As the fire crackled, we asked about his family and where he had come from. He told us that his family was quite religious and that he had not made many choices of which they approved—including being a wilderness guide. He also had not gotten married and had not finished university after six years of trying. And he was not religious—not even, he felt, a Muslim anymore. We asked him about that. He paused for a moment. "Do you want to hear my story?"

He took a drink from the bottle of wine. I could tell that despite his hesitance, he wanted to tell his story. He just needed it to be set apart. It couldn't be told in the normal course of things, among other chatter. He waited and let the night settle around us. The candles wavered in the circle they created.

"When I was a kid, I always went to these religious camps in the summer. The point of the camps was to memorize the Qur'an—there is a lot of the Qur'an to memorize—and I was good at it. You earned prizes, and they had swimming and activities. I had an uncle who was a judge in Islamic law. I always admired him, and I wanted to be like him. So I kept going, every summer, to the camp. The people who ran the camp, they liked me, and when I got a little older, they asked me if I wanted to go to this Islamic school that met not only in the summer. I said sure. So I started going during the rest of the year too.

"One day when I was about sixteen, the people who ran that school took a small group of us down into the basement of the mosque where there was a Ping-Pong table and a TV. They said, 'What we are about to show you, you can never talk about, ever, to anyone.'"

Monther could see that written on the DVD cover, in Arabic, were the words "Russian hell." They put the DVD into the player, and the television flickered into a video. Monther saw Al-Qaeda fighters in

Afghanistan who were holding four Russian soldiers hostage. The soldiers were tied up in a line. The fighters cried, "Allah Akbar!" and slit the throats of the four Russian soldiers.

"To this day," Monther said, "I can still hear the sound of the gurgling in their throats as they fought for life, fought to breathe. For two days, I didn't do anything. I didn't tell anyone. I was just trying to think what to do. Then I decided to tell my father. I told him what they had shown me in that video. He said, 'If you ever go back there, I will break both your legs.' So I never went back, but I started to question everything. Was this Islam? Was this what it taught? If it is a religion, it should unify and not divide, but why were Muslims killing Muslims—in Afghanistan and Yemen and Iraq? None of it made any sense to me. My questions got too big, and I just couldn't believe anymore."

Now Monther called himself Abu Shams not only because Shams can be either a boy's name or a girl's name and he likes the nonbinary nature of it but also because *shams* means "the sun." He showed us the totem around his neck, an ancient symbol of the sun. He is a devotee of the sun, he said. He goes into the natural world to heal himself, and now he has started taking other young people with him, knowing that nature has the power to heal them too. I wondered if he would call his search a search for atonement—the power to unify and not divide.

4.

The next day, we broke camp and continued downstream into steeper and steeper regions of the canyon. As we hiked, Monther pointed out insects that were clinging to rocks. They looked like bodies poised to jump if you touched them. I peered closer.

"They're dead," Monther said. "Go ahead; you can touch them."

I picked the papery body off the rock where it looked as if it were about to leap and held it in my hand. It was weightless, empty.

"It's the . . . how do you say it?" Monther asked. "The evolution of the dragonfly? The back is open and the dragonfly flies out. Not evolution. Life cycle. It is like a butterfly, when it is a caterpillar and it becomes a . . ."

"Cocoon?"

"Cocoon. That is the cocoon of the dragonfly."

I stared at the beautiful, empty body. A dragonfly chrysalis. Around us, we saw many living dragonflies, and now that Monther had pointed them out to us, I also saw many shells clinging to these rocks "as if" alive.

In the *Life of Mary of Egypt*, Zosimas comes to Mary two more times after their first encounter. The first time, he follows her instructions to meet him on the banks of the Jordan with communion. The story says that during the year between their first meeting and their second, he did not stop thinking about her and longing for her. He asked God to "show him again the one face he desired. He felt vexed thinking of the length of a year, wishing that one year could become a day."

On the day they had agreed to meet, he went down to the shore with a basket of soaked lentils and dried fruit along with a flask of wine and the bread of Holy Communion. She did not come for a long time, and he began to despair, thinking he had missed the time or the day or he had been late and she had left. He began to think his own "wretchedness" prevented her from coming.

Then finally he saw her on the far side of the river. She began to walk across the water toward him. He bowed down, and this annoyed her. Even while she was walking across the water, she called out to him to please stop with the bowing routine.

When she reached the other side, they said the liturgy together. Then she gave him the "kiss of love on his mouth" and "partook of the life-giving mysteries." Her eyes filled with tears.

He showed her the basket that he had prepared for her—the simple food of monks, but a taste of civilization nonetheless. She touched the lentils with her fingers, almost with affection, and brought a few to her lips. He bowed down again and touched her feet and asked her to pray for him. "But he did not hold for long the one who would not be held."

The second time, he followed her instructions again. This time, she told him to go to the place where they had first met. It was another long journey, and once again, when he arrived he didn't see her. "Looking around right and left and turning around everywhere, his sight was like the experienced hunter who looks everywhere for his most sweet prey to capture." In the wilderness, there was only stillness. Maybe there was the sound of the wind. Maybe he heard a Tristram's starling. Finally, he saw her, lying dead and facing east, as if her body had been arranged by some unseen hand in preparation for burial. That's when he also saw a note written for him on the earth, telling him her name and asking for his prayers. She had died deep in the wilderness that she loved.

Zosimas was determined to bury her, but he scratched and clawed at the hard ground and got nowhere. "How will you dig a pit, you poor man," he said to himself, "without a tool?" When he had worked away without success, he suddenly looked up and saw a lion standing over the remains of Mary, "licking the soles of her feet," with tenderness, I imagine.

The lion and Zosimas buried her body together, and then they both departed—the lion into the wilderness, the monk to the monastery to spend the rest of his life telling this story.

5.

All day as Monther, Peter, and I hiked out of the wadi, I thought about the dragonfly chrysalis. At every turn, our hike grew more beautiful: the sandstone cliffs, the cascading oleander, the unhurried stream, and the light reflecting off of it. I had fallen and lost my sunglasses in the stream. My feet and my tailbone hurt. My arms and legs were scraped up from scrambling over ancient coral. My pace was slow. Peter often waited for me at tricky places where the water was high and offered a hand to help me cross.

At first, I thought of the chrysalis as a symbol of death; it is the shell from which the spirit has flown. But then I thought about the whole of Mary's journey, from various kinds of emptinesses to new life found here in the wilderness: the emptiness of her life in Alexandria, perhaps; the empty tomb at the Church of the Holy Sepulchre; the deep emptiness of the desert. The chrysalis is not a symbol of death even though it is an empty shell. It is a symbol of transition—it vivifies the exact means by which a creature of the water makes a brief foray onto land before becoming a creature of the air. It is a symbol for the journey, for the risky business of leaving the old ways behind and taking up something new—something that darts and shimmers and lives.

At sunset, we finally emerged onto the Dead Sea plain again, and the light turned the sandstone almost golden in color. We had lost all track of time, and Jawad and our driver had nearly sent a search party in to look for us. When we emerged, we saw the worried looks on the faces of our hosts, and I was a little embarrassed for the sense I'd had of lingering in another world.

But the Jordanians quickly forgave us and delivered us to a place where we could shower. We were served another plate of delicious chicken and rice, and then we packed up for the airport.

"I found her," a little voice inside me whispered and danced, darting like a dragonfly.

"When you found her, what did you ask her?" said another voice.

"I asked her how to be fully alive."

"What did she say?"

"Be like the dragonfly."

EPILOGUE

TRANSLATED

It is never a mistake to go in search of what one requires. Never.
                                            —Clarissa Pinkola Estés

We entreat you, make us fully alive.
        —Sarapion of Themius, a prayer from fourth-century Egypt

RETURN

Many hours and several airplanes later, we returned to Leadville. I
returned to my icon at home in my window, and I placed in front of
her the small gifts I had collected along the way. There were a few leaves
of the cassia tree and an herb that grows abundantly in Nubia, the
name of which I don't remember. There was one of the tiny flowers from
the Judean Desert that improbably grows amid all that rock, a small
chunk of mosaic that had fallen to the ground at the site of Mary of
Egypt, and a handmade bracelet that had been dropped by a tourist on

the floor of the Church of the Holy Sepulchre. It wasn't exactly the pilgrim treasures of old—the drops of holy oil and tiny terra-cotta flasks of holy water. But ancient pilgrims had pocketed pebbles and pinches of dirt from holy sites, scrapes of candlewax, blades of grass, pieces of wood, and bits of plaster—all to symbolize and make concrete a sense of the holy that could be carried with them. I had essentially done the same, and I put these before my Mary so she could see what treasures I had found along the way.

Meanwhile, Ali was on her way back to Colorado for the long road—a much harder and longer pilgrimage with even fewer guarantees. Her road was toward surgery and chemotherapy, experimental drugs, months of homelessness, and a future as uncertain as any ascetic's has ever been. As I began to clamber among the ruins of my old life now that Ali had left Leadville to live closer to the hospital, I didn't know what to carry forward and what to leave behind.

I had gone in search of Mary of Egypt convinced that I was going in search of a legend, a great "as if." Before I had left home, I put quotation marks around all of it. Mary of Egypt "lived" in the fifth century—or maybe the sixth or the fourth. The "record" of her existence was flimsy at best, and surely Sophronius got most of it wrong.

But by the time I had walked the path, crossed the Jordan River, and found myself in the company of thousands of previous pilgrims—albeit ghostly ones from another time—I no longer thought of her as a legend. She had lived. And she had left her mark, just not in the books of American scholarship. That she was remembered was a strange kind of miracle. The palace of the lady—that ancient joke and ancient homage, still alive. And even so, she was every bit as ephemeral and every bit as wild as I had imagined. A dragonfly. A woman who had come to peace with the wind and the sand and the sun, a person who had become light.

ANOTHER WILDERNESS

The hospital room on the eleventh floor of the Anschutz Medical Center in Denver was not exactly like the brown hills of the Palestinian desert or the ancient seabed of the Jordanian wilderness. But I felt on the boundary between two biblical kingdoms anyway. This place was a desert. It was like being inside the dragonfly chrysalis: not much to see here.

Ali lay on the hospital bed in the center of the room as undone as I had ever known her to be. The old life was not falling away gently like an unnecessary layer of clothing. It was shedding itself as if possessed by some centripetal force, flinging its shards at us while we ducked for cover.

The surgery to remove the cancer had been extensive, but she had healed well, everywhere except the colon. From the beginning, she had intense and terrifying pain in her abdomen. Then two infections struck. After a few rounds of chemotherapy, her weight falling rapidly, the doctors had discovered a blockage in her colon caused by her body's own scar tissue. She had to have another surgery, even though she was not fully recovered from the first. The intensity of these blows was, it was obvious, eroding her will to live.

I had flown in from Chicago. A polar vortex had shut Chicago down, and I had ridden in a cab through empty streets to an airport where only a few planes could take off that day because it was too cold for workers to stand on the tarmac. I had arrived in the much balmier Denver at her hospital room and did nothing more than pull up a stool and sit.

"This is hell," she whispered to me through the tubes.

I tried to remember what I had learned from that other desert. Survival 101: Look for the oleander. Oleander is the beautiful plant that spills out over cliff walls to dramatize the presence of pure water. It tells you, by its beauty, where to look for the most basic need you have. Mother hadn't mentioned that it is also highly toxic. It can poison you, but it was also used in the Middle Ages to treat cancer. It is resistant to drought and can thrive where there is little water—a wild, wild plant. As a "desert rose," it has been considered throughout history to represent the feminine face of God.

I looked into Ali's face, drawn and gaunt. Her long red hair had begun to fall out a few weeks previously, and rather than watch it fall out a little at a time, she shaved the rest of it off. We joked that she bore more than a passing resemblance to Dobby the house-elf from Harry Potter.

At the least, "look for the oleander" reminds me to look for the beauty but not to be sentimental about it. It's not the beauty, in the end, that you want, but the presence of pure water it reveals.

We looked out from the west-facing windows toward the mountains and watched the light. For Ali, sunrise was the easiest light to pay attention to: light leading to light. We sat as light spread behind the mountains and then covered them with early morning alpine glow. They turned rose and gold as the sun danced on them.

But sunset, with light leading to dark, was still much harder, just as she had written to me when I was in Egypt. It was equally beautiful—colors spread across the mountains, clouds gathered and drifted apart. Gold light would sometimes fill the room for a few minutes. Every day the light stayed a little bit longer. But sunset intensified fears. It brought us all of the "what ifs." It conjured hopelessness, like some evil spirit coming to take away our last bit of meaning and will.

But growing darkness was never the last word. There was always another day and a day after that. We had days to practice; Ali had days to recover, days in which health seemed just around the corner, and days when it was nowhere in sight. It was life, and we were going to have to live it like a walk through the wilderness, without guarantees.

DIE AND BECOME

To move from old life to new life is a struggle. Think how strange a drag-onfly nymph must feel as it is compelled out of the water—its com-fortable home for all of its life—to undergo a complete transformation into a creature of the air. First it has to split open. Then it is exposed to the air in a new bright-green suit—vulnerable to this new reality, hang-ing upside down. No wonder it clings to its old body while the process of growing wings takes place. It does not choose this transformation. Who would want it? The water was fine. There was plenty to eat. The dragon-fly nymph, with monstrous jaws, had a lot of power down there, below the surface.

The new dragonfly clings to the old body, which clings to the rock. Then it grows wings so clear they seem to be made of water. The wings harden, and then clinging no longer serves its purpose, and the dragonfly—one of the first creatures on the earth ever to fly—lets go.

Mary's journey was like the dragonfly's. She left her home, compelled by something she could not name, and learned to rise into the air. She grew wings, the text says, and learned to talk to the air. No less than a metamorphosis.

Those who say Mary cannot be imitated perhaps have not yet seen the chrysalis clinging to the rock face and noticed the dragonfly darting around them. When I said yes to the calling to follow Mary, I consented to an inner journey as well as an outer journey. And I had been met—as Zosimas was, as Mary was. God does not, as Zosimas said, despise anyone.

But new life is ephemeral. It can't quite be pointed to, examined. New life is emergent, not yet.

FULLY ALIVE

When I look at my icon of Mary now, I see the old woman, the Wild Woman, depicted there in myself. We are of the same "earth and ashes and flesh." To look through her as she looks at the sky is to look through me toward the same sky. It is at once an X-ray inward to the bones and a telescope outward to the stars.

The tradition of the desert mothers and fathers says that if we go far enough into the desert, including the desert of ourselves, we find Eve—an old woman now. She has seen everything. She has done everything. She has survived everything and found the pure water hiding in the rock. She now lives with an unexpected lightness in her limbs and in her step, as if the flesh she carried so far is no longer a burden to her. She has found new ground—ground that was once a torrent. When she prays, she rises.

> Amma, desert companion
> Bridge across the sky
> Sky's sister
> Today, I bring you a sprig of juniper
> A little sage, the dried husk of an aster.
> Teach me, I ask, to be fully alive.

ACKNOWLEDGMENTS

I have many people to thank for helping me complete an adventure like this.

Thank you to my traveling companions, Michele Johnson and Peter Frykholm.

Thank you Arianne Zwartjes for pointing me to Yehia El Decken, without whom the journey might never have begun.

Thank you Yehia El Decken and Holiday Tours for creative and constant help.

Thank you Mohamed Abbas, Abu Bakr Hussein Said (Mido), and family for hospitality, open-heartedness, and help all along the way in Egypt.

Thank you Dan Koski for time, generosity, wisdom, and kindness on the subject of Mary of Egypt and perspective on contemporary issues.

Thank you everyone at the Tantur Ecumenical Institute for good food, good conversation, and loads of advice.

Thank you Jacqueline Mozoyer, the librarian at Tantur, for books, conversation, curiosity, and wisdom.

Thank you Anna Koulouris for your remarkable ability to open doors of all kinds and your gracious use of that ability for me. And thank you Archbishop Isidoros of Hierapolis and the Greek Orthodox Patriarchate of Jerusalem for finding the key and allowing me to see the Chapel of Mary of Egypt.

Thank you Suhair Ghanim, the Siraj Center, and George Giacaman for helping us arrange and complete our "Walk in Palestine."

Thank you Naftali Moses for your gracious hospitality in Israel.

Thank you Robert Smith for all kinds of good advice, including guiding me to Razzouk Tattoos.

Thank you Umm Fares and the Mudhouse Guesthouse at the Aqbat Jaber Refugee Camp.

Thank you Experience Jordan, Jawad Nayef Aburumman, Monther Altiti, and Matt Loveland.

Thank you to all who listened to my story along the way and offered their wisdom, advice, driving skills, pack-schlepping, generosity, and humor. Live hearts, all!

On this side of the world:

Thank you Chris and Rachel Huebner and Peter Dula for guidance and early interest in the project, enough to make me think it wasn't insane.

Thank you Tom Johnson for oh so many things, but not least for free weekly Skype lessons in Greek and for the process of translating the *Life of Mary of Egypt* together. Those hours are precious to me.

Thank you Mary Green, not only for the icon, which has guided me constantly, but for conversation, deep listening, and care for this ancient tradition.

Thank you Susan Holman for good conversation about Sophronius and his environment.

Thank you Joanne Wyckoff, my agent, for engaging with the project so deeply from the first.

Thank you Mara Naselli for our now almost thirty-year conversation about writing.

Thank you Lisa Morton, Susan Fishman, and Luz Escalera for making the Community Meal a place where the stranger can be welcomed.

Thank you Ali Lufkin—I hope this book is like a very long thank-you note.

Thank you Samuel Frykholm for allowing your mom to go off wandering while you were in the midst of your own big adventure.

Thank you Lil Copan. Thank you for believing, for pastries in Chama, and for your care of each individual word.

APPENDICES

GLOSSARY OF PEOPLE, PLACES, AND TERMS

abaya—a full-length outer garment worn by some Muslim women

al-Eizariya—the contemporary name of Bethany, a city in the West Bank

Alexandria—the second largest city in Egypt on the Mediterranean coast

Amma—the Greek word for "mother," often used to refer to female ascetics

ascetic—a person who practices self-deprivation or extreme self-discipline, usually for spiritual purposes

Aswan—the capital of the Egyptian state of Nubia

Bedouin—a member of traditional nomadic Arab tribes

Bethany—the city in which Jesus's friends Mary, Martha, and Lazarus were said to be from; now called al-Eizariya

burka—a long, loose garment covering the whole body from head to feet, worn in public by many Muslim women

Byzantium—a late ancient Christian kingdom, the continuation of the Holy Roman Empire into the Middle Ages from roughly the fifth century AD until 1453, when it was subsumed into the Ottoman Empire

Chapel of St. James—a small chapel off of the main outer courtyard of the Church of the Holy Sepulchre in Jerusalem

Church of the Holy Sepulchre—the church built over the site where Jesus is said to have been raised from the dead; the traditional center of Christianity

Gregory of Nyssa—a Christian saint who served as the bishop of Nyssa in the fourth century

hagiography—a saint's biography

Hassa—an island in the Nile in the Egyptian region of Nubia

Jaffa—the ancient coastal port on the Mediterranean that is now part of Tel Aviv

Jerome—a fourth- and fifth-century church father who lived in Bethlehem

John Moschos—a sixth-century monk who wrote a book called *The Spiritual Meadow*

kaffiyeh—a headscarf traditionally worn by Arab men

Kidron Valley—the valley that runs from the eastern side of Jerusalem through the Judean Desert in the West Bank toward the Dead Sea; the site of Mar Saba, an ancient Christian monastery

kippah—a small round hat worn by many Jewish men

Kom el-Dikka—an archaeological site in Alexandria, Egypt, that contains extensive ruins from the Roman and Byzantine eras

Life of Mary of Egypt—a text from the seventh century attributed to Sophronius of Jerusalem about an otherwise unknown desert ascetic

Mar Saba—a Christian monastery in the Kidron Valley, founded in the fifth century

Mary of Egypt—a Christian saint who was a hermit in the Jordanian wilderness for most of her life

Miryam al Masreya—the Arabic name for Mary of Egypt

Monastery of St. Anthony—the oldest Christian monastery in the world, located in Egypt, founded in the fourth century

Monastery of St. George—Christian monastery in the Wadi Qelt, founded in the early sixth century

Monastery of St. Gerasimos—Christian monastery near the Jordan River, founded in the fifth century

Nubia—the southernmost region of contemporary Egypt

Patrologia Graeca—a collection of writings of the earliest Christian ascetics, many of whom lived in the desert (*Life of Mary of Egypt* is collected in this document.)

Seheyl—an island in the Nile in the Egyptian region of Nubia

shawarma—a Middle Eastern treat of grilled meat

Sophronius—a sixth- to seventh-century Christian monk, writer, and thinker who became the Patriarch of Jerusalem at the end of his life and turned the keys to Jerusalem over to Arab invaders in 636

Tantur Ecumenical Institute—the research and retreat center where I stayed in Jerusalem

Theotokos—literally "God-bearer," a common name for Mary the Mother of God in Orthodox Christianity

wadi—the Arabic term for a valley, ravine, or channel that is dry except in the rainy season

Wadi al Hasa—the ancient border between the biblical kingdoms of Moab and Edom

Wadi Qelt—the valley that runs from near Jerusalem to Jericho along an ancient Roman aqueduct

Zamalek—an island in the Nile in the city of Cairo, currently a trendy place with shops and boutiques

Zosimas—the monk who discovered Mary of Egypt in the desert and became devoted to her

LIFE OF MARY OF EGYPT

A Translation by Thomas F. Johnson and Amy Frykholm

Who from prostitution became a holy ascetic in the Jordanian desert as was written down by the holy Sophronius, patriarch of Jerusalem.

—*Patrologia Graeca* 87:3693–726

PROLOGUE

It is good to conceal the secret of a king, but it is good to acknowledge and reveal the works of God, and with fitting honor to acknowledge him.*

This the angel said to Tobit when his sight was returned to him after a time of blindness. He was saved through many dangers because of his devotion.

Not to keep the secrets of a king is dangerous, but consider what it means to keep secret the wondrous works of God. Such secret keeping endangers the soul.

I fear being silent about divine things. I listened to the parable of the servant who received a talent from his master and buried it in the earth. I too perceive the danger of hiding gifts so they cannot be useful.† So I

---

* Tobit 12:7.

† Matthew 25:18.

will not be silent about a holy tale that has come down to me. Let no one disbelieve me. Do not think that I am exaggerating or merely relating marvels. For I would not give false testimony or corrupt a word of a story that pertains to the works of God. If you have lowly thoughts about the incarnate word of God, you will also not believe what is said here.

If there are those who have seen this writing and find this amazing story too difficult to believe, may God have mercy on them, for they have given in to the weak nature of human beings and find it difficult to accept miracles.

But now I relate the account of an event that took place in this generation about a holy man, who from childhood had spoken and acted in the way of divine things. This account should not lead to unbelief for those readers who do not think that such miracles can occur in this generation, for, just as Solomon taught, the grace of the Father makes friends and prophets for God in every generation.*

CHAPTER ONE

There was a certain man in one of the monasteries of Palestine, adorned in word and in life, and from the cradle was brought up in monastic character and practices. Zosimas was the name of this monk. (And let no one consider me to be speaking about that Zosimas once charged with being a heretic. For these men are very different from one another, even if they have the same name.) This Zosimas was indeed orthodox and lived as a monk in one of the old monasteries. He pursued every outward form of asceticism. He accustomed himself to every kind of self-discipline and followed every rule that had been handed down by those who knew and had trained in this arena of spiritual struggle. He also kept many

---

* Wisdom 7:27.

rules that he himself thought up as he sought to subordinate the flesh to the spirit. And in this goal, he did not miss the mark. This monk was a symbol of spirituality, and many often came from monasteries near and far to be molded and trained in self-discipline by his teaching.

A model of practice, this monk also did not neglect the study of the Word of God. He studied in both sleeping and rising and while he did work with his hands, from which he earned his daily bread. If you wish to know the true nourishment that he tasted, it was to sing psalms at all times and always to study holy things. Some said this holy man was certainly worthy to receive divine visions. As Christ said, those who purify themselves and exercise vigilance in the eye of their souls will see God. They will receive divine illumination as a foretaste of the good things awaiting them.*

Zosimas said that from his mother's arms he had been given to this monastery, and since then, he followed the ascetic path until he was fifty-three years old. At this time, he became troubled by the thought that he had been perfected and no longer needed the teaching of others. He said to himself, "Where is there a monk in the world who has surpassed me? Who has proven greater than me in practice? Can I find anyone in the desert ahead of me in the practice of contemplation?"

While he was thinking these things, someone came near to him and said, "Zosimas, you have struggled well and you have followed the ascetic path. But there is no human who is perfected. Greater is the struggle before you than the one that has passed, even if none of you know it. In order that you might learn how many roads there are to salvation, go from the land of your kindred and from the house of your fathers, just as Abraham did.† Go to the monastery that is near the river Jordan."

---

* Matthew 5:8.

† Genesis 12:1.

The monk went immediately, following this command to go out from the monastery where he had been since childhood. He made his way to the most holy Jordan River, led by the one who had ordered him to go to that monastery where God had commanded him to be. He knocked on the gate and was met by the monk who guarded the gate. The guard made him known to the leader of the monastery, who observed his appearance and his reverent character.

Zosimas bowed down in the custom of monks and then the leader asked him, "Brother, where have you come from and why have you come to these humble monks?" Zosimas answered, "I do not think it is necessary to say where I have come from. I am indebted to grace, O Father. I have come because I have heard concerning you many honorable and praise-worthy things, things that have the power to bring a soul home to Christ, our God."

The leader said to him, "God alone, brother, heals human weakness; God teaches both you and us the things of the divine will, and God will lead us to the right path. For we cannot help each other unless we turn within ourselves continually and are vigilant concerning our own discernment. Then we can do what is necessary, with God's help.

"However, since indeed, as you said, the love of God has moved you to visit these humble monks, remain with us if indeed you have arrived for this reason. And the Good Shepherd, who gave his life as a ransom for us, will feed all of us by the grace of the Spirit. His own lambs he calls by name."*

Zosimas prostrated himself and asked for a blessing; then saying, "Amen," he remained at that monastery.

Zosimas saw that these monks shone—both by practice and by contemplation. They burned with the Holy Spirit and served the Holy One.

---

* John 10:3.

Their psalmody was unceasing; they stood vigil all night. They always had handiwork in their hands and psalms in their mouths. They did not use words idly. They were so unconcerned with the things of this world that they did not even know the names of the annual revenues that were counted and gathered. Instead, each of them hastened to mortify the body, as they each had already died to the world and did not exist to those outside of the monastery. They partook of the inexhaustible nourishment of Holy Scriptures. They nourished the body by necessity only, with bread and water. Each one burned ardently with divine love.

Zosimas observed these things, as he said, and was built up greatly as he strove to grow on his own path and to seek with his fellow travelers to re-create divine paradise.

The time of the traditional fasts approached during which Christians purified themselves in preparation for the veneration of Christ's sufferings and resurrection. Now the gate of the monastery was never opened so that these monks might have undisturbed ascetic practice. It was only opened when a monk had some vital necessity. This meant that this desert monastery was not only inaccessible to most of its neighboring monks; it was also unknown.

This monastery had a certain rule that it had kept from the beginning, and I think this was the reason why God led Zosimas to this very monastery. This particular rule and how it was kept, I will now say.

On the first Sunday in Lent, the divine liturgy was performed, as was the custom, and each of the monks shared in the life-giving mysteries and sacraments, and each also partook of a little nourishment. After this, they gathered in the chapel and performed long prayers and sufficient kneelings. Then they bid farewell to one another, and embracing their leader, each one prostrated himself and asked to receive a blessing in order to have it from a fellow and experienced struggler for the spiritual combat in front of them.

Then the gate of the monastery was opened, and singing in unison the hymn, "The Lord is my light and my salvation; whom shall I fear?

The Lord is the stronghold of my life; of whom shall I be afraid?"* they all went out of the monastery. They often left one or two behind to act as guards of the monastery, not to protect the things that were lying there (for nothing there could be easily taken by thieves), but in order not to leave the chapel without liturgy.

Each one of the monks provisioned himself just as he was able and just as he pleased. Each one provided himself with food for the body, as he deemed necessary: one with dried figs, another with dates, a different one with lentils soaked in water, another with nothing except his own body and the rags thrown around him. He fed when nature demanded it on the plants growing in the wilderness.

There was a rule that each one kept like an unchangeable law: each was not to know where the others went, how they practiced their disciplines, or how they spent their time. When they crossed over the Jordan, they immediately withdrew from one another, and they made the desert their city.† No one came near another, and if one saw another coming toward him, he turned at once in another direction in order to avoid him. So each lived for himself and for God, always chanting psalms and nourishing himself with whatever was at hand.

When the days of the fasting were completed, they returned to the monastery on the Sunday of the feast that is celebrated traditionally with palms. Each returned having sown seeds through his own travail, each knowing in his conscience how he had labored. No one asked anything at all of the others or how their struggle had gone. This was the monastery rule, and in this way, it was well accomplished. For each of them, while in the wilderness, struggled under God the judge, not to please others or to make a show of their self-control. They sought their own freedom. Those

---

* Psalm 26 (27):1.

† The phrase comes from the *Life of Anthony the Great* by Athanasius of Alexandria.

things done for the sake of pleasing other people not only do not benefit the person practicing them; they can also bring about harm.

So Zosimas, by the usual rule of the monastery, crossed the Jordan, having supplied himself with small provisions for the need of the body and the same tattered garment with which he clothed himself. He kept the rule. He made time for food as nature required, and he slept by night on the ground, lying down and getting a little sleep wherever he was when the time of evening overtook him. At dawn, very early, he set out to walk again, always staying on the move with constant energy.

He came into a desire, he said, to go into the deeper desert, hoping to find a father in it who would be able to help him toward the thing he was striving for. And indeed, with energy, he continued the journey, as one hurrying toward some eminent and famous inn.

On his twentieth day on the road, when the sixth hour came, he stood for a moment, and gazing to the east, he said his customary prayer. He did this at appointed times of the day: he would interrupt the progress of the journey, rest from labor, stand to sing psalms, and bend the knee to pray.

While he was chanting psalms and looking to heaven, praying at the sixth hour with an unceasing eye, he saw to his right side the shadow of a human body appear. At first he was troubled, supposing that it was a demonic phantasm, and he started to tremble.[*] By making the sign of the cross, he shook off this fear. When his prayer ended, he turned and in fact saw someone naked walking toward the south. The one he saw was black in body as if burned by the sun and had hair that was white as if it were

---

[*] "The monk approached his desert dwelling place with a mixture of excited anticipation, because it was the place of God, and nervous anxiety, because it was the home of devils, wild beasts, and the Saracens." Binns, *Ascetics and Ambassadors*, 225. But interestingly, in this story, there are no demons, just like there are no villains. The struggle is with the self and the self alone.

wool, and this hair was short, not even reaching the neck. These things Zosimas observed with joy. Filled with the unexpected pleasure of seeing someone, he began to run toward the part of the desert where the one he saw hastened. He rejoiced with an unspeakable joy, for in all the days he had been in the desert, he had never seen a human figure or an animal or a bird or any terrestrial form or even a shadow. He sought to know who or what sort of thing he had seen, hoping that he might become a witness to great things.

When the one he had seen perceived Zosimas coming at a distance, it began to flee, running farther into the inner part of the desert. But Zosimas, forgetting his old age and not counting the exhaustion of his journey, exerted himself and pressed on to catch up to the one fleeing him. One was pursuing, but the other was being pursued. Zosimas ran faster, and so after a little while, he got closer to the fleeing one. When he had approached so that his voice could be heard from a distance, he began to cry out with tears, "Why are you fleeing an old man and a sinner, O servant of the one true God? Wait for me, whoever you are, in the name of God who is the God of this desert in which you dwell. Wait for me, the weak and unworthy, for the sake of the hope and reward of your labor. Stop and give a blessing to this old man. God does not ever detest anyone." Zosimas said this with tears as both of them ran toward a place where a torrent had left a trace in a dry riverbed. (It does not seem to me that there ever was a torrent in this place, for how could a torrent appear in this land? But the place had such a setting.)

CHAPTER TWO

When they had arrived at this place, the fleeing one went down one side of the ravine and again up the other side, while Zosimas, weary and no longer able to run, stood on the other side of the dry streambed and added tears upon tears and lamentation upon lamentation so that anyone in the area could hear his wailings from a distance.

Then the fleeing one cried out: "Father Zosimas, forgive me, in God's name. I am not able to turn and be seen by you to your face, for I am a woman and naked, even as you see, and I have the shame of my uncovered body. But if indeed you are willing to grant a sinner-woman one favor, throw me the rag that is around you so that in it I will clothe the weakness of women, and I will turn to you and provide for your wishes."

A shudder and strike of ecstasy hit Zosimas, he said, when he heard her call him by name. For the man was sharp and most wise, and he saw that she could never have said that concerning someone she had never seen unless she had been gifted with foresight. She clearly shone with that gift.

Swiftly he did what had been asked of him and removed the old and torn garment. He threw it to her while standing with averted eyes. She took it and covered what of her body she could. She turned then to Zosimas and said to him, "Why do you seek, Father Zosimas, to gaze upon a sinful woman? What do you so long to hear or to see from me that you are willing to undergo such a labor?"

But he bent his knees to the ground and asked her to bless him according to the custom. She threw herself before him as well. They both lay on the ground, each one asking for a blessing from the other, and for an interval of many hours, there was nothing to hear from either of them except "Bless me." Finally, the woman said to Zosimas, "Father Zosimas, it is fitting for you to bless and to pray, for you are a priest worthy to be honored. For many years you have stood before the holy altar, and often you have been a celebrant of the divine gifts."

These words threw Zosimas into greater fear and anguish. Trembling, the monk became drenched in sweat. With broken and constricted breath, he said to her, "It is clear to me, O spiritual Mother, from this situation, that you have traveled to God and you have died to the world.

It is clear that you have a charism that allows you to call me by name and to say that I am a priest even though you have never seen me. And since grace is made known not from high rank but by the way of a spiritual life, bless me according to God and share prayer with the one who is begging for your help."

Yielding to him at last, the woman said, "Blessed be God, who cares for the salvation of all people and all souls."

Zosimas said, "Amen," and they both rose from their knees. The woman again said to the monk, "Why have you come to me, O man? Why have you come to see a woman naked of all goodness? Since doubtless the grace of the Holy Spirit has guided you for some important service, tell me, how do the Christian folk conduct themselves today? How are the kings? How are the shepherds of the church?"

Zosimas said to her, "In brief, Mother, through your holy prayers, Christ has granted to all a steadfast peace. But receive from an old monk an unworthy supplication, and when you pray for the whole world, pray also for me, a sinner, so that my time in the desert might not be a fruitless one.'"*

She answered him, "As I have said, Father Zosimas, it is your job to pray for me and for all. You are a worthy priest, and this has been chosen for you. But in obedience to you, I will willingly do what you ask."

She turned to the east, and raising her eyes to heaven and extending her hands, she began to pray, whispering softly. Her voice was not audible, and Zosimas could not hear her words. He stood, as he said, trembling and silent, bending his head toward the earth. But he swore,

---

* Zosimas's words here indicate that the monastic world of Mary's time saw itself as intimately connected to the Christian empire. They were both aware of the ways that the empire could affect the life of the monasteries but also believed that their work of prayer in the desert sustained the empire itself. See Binns, *Ascetics and Ambassadors.*

with God as his witness, that this is what he saw. As she prayed, he lifted his head and saw her raised up about one cubit from the earth, hanging in the air. He fell to the ground, struck by even greater fear, and was exceedingly agonized and dared utter nothing, only saying over and over to himself, "God have mercy." He thought that she might indeed be a demonic spirit after all, only pretending to pray.

The woman turned to him and, raising him up, said, "Why, Father, do you have these troubling thoughts that have scandalized you about me? Why do you think I am a spirit who has come into existence and uttered a prayer falsely? Be assured, O man, that I am a sinful woman who has nevertheless been protected by Holy Baptism. A spirit I am not, but earth and ashes and altogether flesh, nothing spiritual at all." Saying these things, she sealed herself with the sign of the cross on her forehead and eyes, lips, and chest. She said, "Father Zosimas, let God deliver us from the evil one and from his attack because he is strong against us."

Hearing and observing these things, the monk again threw himself on the ground and seized her feet, with tears saying, "I implore you by the name of Christ our God, born from the virgin for whose sake you are clothed in this nakedness and for whose sake you have worn out your fleshly life, hide nothing from your servant. Who are you and where have you come from and when and by what means have you dwelt in this desert? Hide nothing from me that pertains to you, but tell me everything so that the great things of God might become clear. *Wisdom hidden and treasure invisible, what good comes from either?** as it has been written. Tell me everything, by God. Do not say it for the sake of boasting or for a show, but so that you might fulfill me, a sinful and unworthy man. I believe in God in whom you live and have led your life. For this reason I was led into the desert, so that the things pertaining to you might be made clear. It is not in our power to oppose the judgment of God. If it

---

* Wisdom of Jesus Ben Sira 20:30.

was not pleasing to Christ, you and your struggle would not have been seen by anyone, nor would I have had the strength to travel such a road, I who never intended and was not able even to go out of my cell."

After he said these things and more, the woman raised him up and said to him, "I am ashamed, my Father, to tell you my deeds. Forgive me, by God. However, since you have seen my naked body, I will lay bare to you as well my deeds so that you may know with how much shame and degradation my soul has been filled. It is not for the sake of boasting that I am inclined to tell you this story, for what do I have to boast about except having become the chosen vessel of the devil? I know that when I begin this story about myself, you will flee from me as one flees from a snake, not bearing to hear with your ears the outrageous things I have done. I will speak, though, and I will not be silent about anything. I only ask you to swear not to stop praying for me so that I may find mercy in the hour of judgment." While the monk shed unchecked tears, the woman began to tell the story of herself:

"I myself, brother, had Egypt as my homeland. When my parents were living and I reached the age of twelve, I set aside my affection for my family and went to Alexandria. Right from the beginning, I destroyed my virginity, and without self-control I threw myself into the passion of sexual intercourse. I am ashamed to think of it. But now, I will say this thing, briefly, for it seems noble that you may know the state of my passion and my love of pleasure. For seventeen years, forgive me, Father, I continued to devote myself publicly as fuel for debauchery. And it was not in order to receive payment from others, I swear, for many times they wished to pay me. Instead, I did this for my own satisfaction. Do not suppose that I was well off and for that reason did not accept money. I begged to support myself, and often I spun flax so that I could devote myself to insatiable and unchecked lust, to roll in that mud. This to me was life: to make of myself entirely an insult to nature.

"One summer day, I saw Libyan and Egyptian men in a large crowd running to the sea. I asked the person next to me, 'Where are they running to, these men?' He answered, 'They are all going up to Jerusalem for the Exaltation of the Holy Cross, which will take place in a few days.' I said, 'Will they take me with them, if I want to go?' He said, 'If you have the ticket price and money for your expenses, no one will prevent you.' But I said to him, 'Truly, brother, I have no money, not for the ticket price nor for the passage, but even so, I am going to go with them. I am going to go up into one of those boats they have hired, and they will take care of me, even if they don't want to, for I have this body that they will receive instead of passage.'

"This was the reason I wanted to go—my Father forgive me—so that I might have many lovers at the ready for my passion. I shiver, God knows, for defiling both you and the air with my words."

Zosimas, his tears soaking the ground, answered her, "Speak in the name of the Holy One, O my Mother. Speak and do not cut off the flow of such a helpful story."

She took up from where she left off: "The young man heard my shameful words, laughed, and went away. I threw away the distaff, which I happened to be carrying at the time, and I ran to the sea where I had seen the men. I saw some youths standing on the beach, about ten in number or even more, vigorous in their bodies and in their movements. They appeared to me sufficient for the thing I was seeking, as it seemed that other sailors were also getting on board and still others had gone up ahead of them into the boats. Shamelessly, as was my custom, I rushed into the middle of them eagerly. 'Take me where you are going,' I said. 'For I will not be found useless.' Then I said words even more shameful, and I moved everyone to laughter. Seeing the temptation of my shamelessness, they led me up into the prepared ship, and we began our voyage.

"How to narrate the things that happened then, O man? What kind of tongue could declare or ear possibly receive the things that occurred on that boat, the things I forced on those unwilling young men? There is no kind of licentiousness, spoken or unspoken, which I did not teach those miserable ones. I am amazed, my Father, how the sea bore up under my debaucheries. How did the earth not open its mouth and lead me alive into Hades, I who trapped so many souls? But it seems that God was seeking my repentance. For God does not will the death of anyone, but patiently waits for the turning around.

"Thus, with haste, we arrived in Jerusalem. As many days as there were before the feast, I passed time in the same manner in which I had been employed before, but now with even worse things. I was not satisfied by the young men I had at sea and those who had rendered service to me on the road, but there were also many others, citizens and foreigners alike, whom I picked up for this purpose."

CHAPTER THREE

"When the Holy Feast of the Exaltation of the Cross arrived, I was wandering around as before, hunting the souls of young men. At deep dawn, I saw everyone running together toward the church, and I also went running with them. I came with the pilgrims into the outer courtyard of the church. When the Hour of Divine Exaltation came, I struggled to get to the entrance of the church. With the others, I pushed and shoved. I hastened to enter with the crowd. I, poor soul, was trying, with much toil and affliction, to draw near to the inner temple. But every time I stepped on the threshold of the door, while all the others entered unhindered, some divine power stopped me and denied me permission to enter. I was pushed back again and again until I found myself alone in the outer courtyard. I decided that this was happening because I was so weak a woman, so I again elbowed my way forward and pressed toward the door. But I labored in vain. When my wretched foot stepped on the threshold, the others were received with no impediment. But I was not received.

"Three or four times I did this, and I grew weary, no longer able to push and shove. My body was beaten by the violence of my efforts. I gave in, and I withdrew to stand in the corner of the courtyard of the temple. Only then, scarcely, did I begin to perceive the cause of my hindrance in seeing the life-giving wood. I became touched in the eyes of my heart. A saving word showed to me that it was the filthiness of my deeds that closed the entrance to me. I began to cry and to moan and to beat my breast. Groans from the depth of my heart rose up. I saw above the place in which I stood, up high, an icon of the ever-holy *Theotokos*. I said to her steadfastly in contemplation, 'Virgin Queen, who gave birth to the Word-God according to the flesh, I know well that it is not proper or reasonable for me, a filthy being, a prodigal, to gaze upon you, the ever-virgin, the chaste, the one who in body and soul is pure and undefiled. It is just for me, the prodigal, to be hated and abhorred by you, the most pure.

"'Nevertheless, since I have heard that the God whom you bore became human so that he might call sinners to repentance, give help to a lone woman who does not have anyone to help her. Allow me to enter the church. Do not deprive me of seeing the wood on which the God whom you bore into flesh was crucified, his own blood that he has given in ransom for me. Command, O Queen, for the door to open for me so that I might kneel in holy adoration of the divine cross. And to you, the one from whom God was born, I give a trustworthy guarantee that no longer will I insult the flesh through any shameful acts of intercourse, at any time whatsoever. When I gaze upon the wood of the cross of your son, I will immediately bid farewell to the world and all the things of the world. I will go out at once, wherever it is that you will send me and guide me.'

"As I said these things, I received the fire of faith as a kind of assurance. Encouraged by the compassion of the *Theotokos*, I went again and mixed myself with those who were entering the church. No longer was anyone pushing and shoving me, no longer was anything hindering me from entering the door, into which they entered the nave. I was overcome by shivering and amazement, bewildered, confused, trembling. As I came to the door that had before been sealed to me, it was as if all the power that had hindered me now prepared my entrance. I went through the door without trouble, and once inside the holy of holies, I came to the life-giving vision of the cross. I saw the mysteries of God, who is ready to receive the repentant. Throwing myself on the earth and kissing that holy ground, I then ran outside again to my benefactor, the one who had agreed to help me.

"Bending my knee before the virgin and God-bearer, I said, 'You indeed, O good-loving Queen, the one who has shown generosity to me, you the righteous one have not rejected me, the unworthy. I saw the glory that we the profligate cannot rightly see. Glory to God, to the one who through you welcomes the repentance of sinners. What else could I a sinner think or utter? It is now time, Queen, to fulfill the promise that I made. Where you command, now lead me. Be the teacher that leads me on the road to repentance.' As I said this, I heard from a distance a voice cry out, 'If you cross the Jordan, you will find a beautiful rest.' I heard the voice, and I believed that it was for me. I cried out to the *Theotokos*, 'Queen, do not forsake me,' and I went out from the courtyard of the church and started walking away.

"As I went out, someone who had seen me gave me three coins. 'Take this, my Mother,' he said. I took these that were offered to me, and with them, I bought three loaves of bread. This I took as a traveler's provision of blessing. I asked the person from whom I bought the bread, 'Where is the road found, O man, which leads to the Jordan?' And learning which gate of the city leads out in that direction, I set off running. I took to the journey weeping. By asking along the way, I drew near the place by the end of the day. (I guess it had been the third hour of the day when I saw the Cross.) As the sun set, I reached the Church of John the Baptist. Before going down to the river, I first worshipped in the church. Then I washed my face and hands with that holy water. I partook of the unde-filed and life-giving sacrament and ate half a loaf of bread and drank from the Jordan. Then I laid myself down on the earth for the night. The next day, I found a small boat, and I crossed to the other side. Again I asked my guide to lead me wherever it would please her that I should go. I came across this desert, and from that time until now, I have lived far off in exile, and in this wilderness I have made my home waiting for my God, the one who protects those who turn toward him from faint-heartedness and hard winds."

Then Zosimas said to her, "How many years, O my lady, have you lived in this desert?"

The woman answered, "Forty-seven years, I guess, from when I left the holy city."

And Zosimas said, "What did you find or have to eat, O my lady?"

The woman said, "The two and a half loaves of bread that I carried across the Jordan grew dry little by little and petrified, and eating them a little at a time, I survived."

Zosimas said, "And so you passed many years without distress; such a sudden change did not trouble you?"

The woman answered, "And now, Father Zosimas, you bring up a sub-ject that I shudder even to speak of. For if I come now to the memory of the many dangers that I indeed endured and of the fearful thoughts that so greatly troubled me, I am afraid, lest I be thrown by them again."

Zosimas said to her, "Leave nothing out, my lady, that you might report to me. For I begged you once to teach me everything."

She said to him, "Believe me, Father, seventeen years I wandered in this desert, fighting with fierce beasts of wordless desires. Whenever I attempted to partake of food, I desired the meats and fishes of Egypt. I most desired wine to drink. For when I had been in the world, I often indulged in a great deal of wine. But here, I did not even have water to taste. I burned dreadfully, and there was no trial I did not bear. To my mind came all the brothel songs unexpectedly, troubling me dreadfully, and seducing me to sing the odes of demons, whose songs I had learned. Immediately, I wept and beat my breast with my hands. I remembered the agreements I had made when I came into the desert. I thought of the icon of the *Theotokos*, my benefactor. And before her, I mourned, and when I asked, she chased away the thoughts that were running against my wretched soul.

"When I had cried enough and had beaten my breast as much as I could, I saw a light shining everywhere around me. And then a certain steady calmness came like a huge wave over me.

"How again will I describe to you, Father, the sexual thoughts that pushed me? A fire was kindled inside my miserable heart, and the fire burned all through me and drew me toward the desire to embrace men sexually. Immediately, when a thought of this kind struck, I threw myself to the earth and wet the ground with my tears. She came to my side, the one who had pledged herself as my protector. And as I stood in transgression, she meted out punishments according to my transgressions. Not rising up from the earth, I would sometimes pass a whole night and day until that sweet light shone around me and chased away the thoughts that were troubling me. Always, when I sent up the eye of my mind toward my benefactor, asking help for the one in danger out in this sea of a desert, I had help and a companion for my repentance. This is how I went through a seventeen-year period conversing with a myriad of dangers. From then until now, my helper has stood by me in everything and through everything has led me by the hand."

Zosimas said to her, "Did you not need food or clothes?"

She answered him, "After seventeen years, when the loaves of bread of which I told you were used up, I then survived with plants and the rest of the things found in the desert. The garment that I had when I crossed the Jordan fell apart. From the cold and from the heat of the flames of summer, I endured great affliction. I endured the burning heat and froze in the frost. Often I shivered on the ground, having fallen breathless, and remained nearly without moving. Through many hazards and unrelenting trials, I have fought. From then until now, the power of God has guarded my sinful soul and my humble body in many ways. When I think only of how many evils he has delivered me from, I have received food without limit, the hope of my soul's salvation. I feed myself and clothe myself with the word of God who governs all things together. For a person does not live by bread alone.* And with respect to not having shelter, for as many as have taken off the covering of sin, they have sheltered themselves with a rock."†

When Zosimas heard the Scriptures that she called to mind from Moses and Job and also the book of Psalms, he said to her, "Have you read the psalms, O my lady, and other books?"

At hearing this, she smiled gently and said to the monk, "Believe me, O man, I have not seen another person from the time I crossed the Jordan until your face today. Neither beast nor other wild creatures have I seen since I saw this desert. Letters, therefore, I have not yet learned. I have not heard psalms or any other reading. The living and active word of God teaches the person knowledge. This is the end of the narration about me. But just as I did when I began this narration, I now beg you, according to God's incarnate word, to pray for me, this woman of debauchery, by God."

Her message now completed, Zosimas rushed to bow down to the ground, and again with tears the monk cried, "Blessed be God who does great and wondrous things, glorious and extraordinary things, which cannot be numbered. Blessed be God who showed to me such things as God gives to those who live in love and fear. For truly, you do not forsake those who seek you, O God."‡

She grasped the monk, no longer consenting for him to bow down before her, but she said to him, "All these things that you have heard, O man, I beg you in the name of our Savior Christ our God, tell no one until the time when God has released me from the earth. Now go in

---

* Deuteronomy 8:3; Matthew 4:4.

† Job 24:8; cf. 1 Corinthians 10:4.

‡ Psalm 9:10.

peace. You will see me again in the coming year, and you will be seen by me, guarded by the grace of God. According to God, now do these things that I command you: during the Holy Fast this coming year, do not cross the Jordan as you have been accustomed to doing at the monastery."

Zosimas was astonished that she reported the rule of the monastery, and he said nothing except "Glory to God. Great things God gives to those who love him."

She said, "As I said, stay, Father, in the monastery, for nothing good will happen to you if you wish to go out. On the evening of the Holy Meal of Mystery, take for me some of the life-giving body and blood of Christ in a vessel worthy of these mysteries and bring it. Wait, for as long as it takes, on the side of the Jordan nearest to civilization so that when I come, I might partake of these life-giving gifts. For since I left the church of the Forerunner, before I crossed the Jordan, I have not enjoyed this holy thing. Now I long for it with unrestrained desire. I beg you not to fail to hear my request, but bring to me these life-giving and divine mysteries at the hour Christ prepared the divine meal for his disciples. Also to Father John, the leader of the monastery in which you live, say these things: 'Take heed of yourself and of your flock; some things that are being done need to be set straight.' But I do not desire that you tell him these things now, but when God permits you."

Then she added, "Pray for me." She once again ran away into the depths of the desert. Zosimas, bowing and reverencing the ground on which the soles of her feet had stood, praised and thanked God. Then he turned back in joy of both soul and body, glorifying and praising Christ our God. He again crossed the desert, and he reached the monastery on the day appointed for the native monks to return.

Chapter Four

All during the year, he was silent. He dared tell no one anything of the things that he had seen. He offered earnest prayer to God to show him again the one face he desired. He felt vexed thinking of the length of a year, wishing that one year could become a day. When the holy fast arrived, on the first Sunday of Lent, the others went out immediately from their customary prayer singing psalms. But he had come down with a sickness, and because of his fever, he was forced to stay inside. A few days passed, and the sickness went away. Zosimas remembered the holy one saying, "Nothing good would happen to you if you wish to go out of the monastery." So he stayed.

When again the monks returned and the evening of the mystical supper approached, he did the things that had been asked of him. Taking into a little vessel the undefiled body and the precious blood of Christ our God, he put them into a basket along with dried figs and dates and small lentils soaked in water. He departed deep in the evening, and he sat on the shore of the Jordan, awaiting the arrival of the holy woman. Even as he waited and she seemed delayed, Zosimas did not doze but gazed steadily at the desert, waiting to see what he longed to see. The monk said to himself sitting there, "So is it my unworthiness that prevents her from coming? Or is it that she came and not finding me turned back again?" He wept and sighed. He lifted his eyes to heaven and beseeched God, saying, "Do not deprive me, Master. Let me again see what you allowed me to see. Do not let me go away empty carrying my sins into judgment." He prayed these things with tears, and then another thought occurred to him. He said to himself, "What will happen if she comes and there is no boat for her to pass over? How will she cross the Jordan even if she comes to me, the unworthy? Woe to me, the most unworthy. Woe to me, the wretched. Who has deprived me rightly of such goodness?"

As he thought this, lo! he saw the holy woman drawing near. She stood on the side of the river from which she had come. Zosimas stood up rejoicing and celebrating and glorifying God. But he again wrestled with the thought that she would not be able to cross the Jordan. Then he saw her make the sign of the holy cross, sealing the Jordan. There was a full moon that night, as he said. At the same time that she made the sign, she stepped onto the water, and she walked on top of the water toward him.

He wished to bow down, but she cried out as she walked on the water, "What are you doing, Father, you who are a priest and who bear the divine mysteries?" He yielded to her words and remained standing. She stepped out of the water and said to the monk, "Bless me, Father, bless me." He answered her with trembling, for he was astonished at the strange sight. "Surely God truly promised to make all those who purify themselves like himself as much as possible. Glory to you, O Christ our God, who did not refuse my prayers and whose mercy has been shown to me through your servant. Glory to you, O Christ our God, who has shown me how far I am from the measure of perfection." Even as he said this, the woman asked him to say the holy creed of the faith and to begin the Our Father. When these things were finished, she gave the monk the kiss of love on his mouth, according to custom, and she partook of the life-giving mysteries. Then she raised her hand to heaven, sighed deeply with tears, and exclaimed, "Now let your servant depart in peace, O Master, according to your word. For my eyes have seen your salvation."*

Then she said to Zosimas, "Forgive me, Father, but I need to ask you to fulfill another desire of mine. Go now to the monastery, guarded by the grace of God, and next year come again to the streambed where you and I met before. Come by all means, according to God, and again you will see me just as God desires."

He answered her, "I wish I could follow you from now on, and see your holy face always. But do this one thing for an old man, and share this

---

* Luke 2:29.

food that I have brought." He showed her the basket. She touched the lentils with her fingertips and took three grains, which she brought to her mouth, thus being contented with the grace of the Spirit to preserve the purity of her soul. Then she said again to the monk, "Pray, in God's name. Pray for me and remember my story."

He touched the holy one's feet and asked her with tears to pray for the church and for the kingdom and for him. Then he released her and lamented while he departed. He did not dare to hold for long the one who would not be held.

She made the sign of the cross again over the Jordan and stepped onto the water to walk to the opposite bank. The monk returned to the monastery with joy and great trembling but found fault in himself for not having sought to learn the holy one's name. He hoped that he would yet be able to obtain it in the coming year.

A year passed, and he went again to the desert. After he had fulfilled everything required by custom, he ran toward the place where he had seen that strange sight two years before. He traveled a long distance into the desert and came upon some signs showing the place he sought. As he looked left and right and turned in every direction, his sight was like the experienced hunter who looks everywhere for his most sweet prey to capture. But not seeing anything moving, he began to weep, and then lifted his eyes and prayed, "Show me, Master, your inviolate treasure, which you have hidden here in the desert. Show me, I beg you, the angel in the body of whom the world is not worthy." Praying these things, he reached the place where there was a streambed, and he saw to the east the holy one lying dead. She lay with her hands formed across her breast, just as they should be, and her body faced the east, as was customary. He ran up to the feet of the blessed one and washed them with his tears, for he did not dare to touch any other part of her.

Through his tears and chanting of psalms, he began the funerary prayers, and then uttered to himself, "So is it fitting to bury the remains of the holy one? Would not this be pleasing to her?" Saying this, he saw above her head writing impressed into the earth. Written there were the words, "Bury the remains of the humble Mary in this place, Father Zosimas. Render dust to dust, and always pray for me. I came to my end in the month of Pharmuthi, as the Egyptians call it. The Romans call it April, on the very night of the Passion of our Savior after I partook of the divine and mystical meal." Reading this, the old man rejoiced because at last he had learned the name of the holy one. He perceived that just as soon as she had partaken of the divine mysteries at the Jordan, she had come to this place and there she had died. This was the very road Zosimas had traveled over for twenty days. Mary had crossed it in one hour and then departed.

Glorifying God and drenching her body with tears, he said to himself, "It is time, humble Zosimas, to fulfill the task commanded of you. But how will you dig a pit, you poor man, without a tool?" He saw, a little way off, a small piece of wood lying on the ground. Taking it up, he began to dig diligently. But the earth being dry, it would not submit to the labor of the old man. But he went on toiling, with sweat dripping. Then groaning mightily, from the depths of his soul, he looked up and saw a huge lion standing at the remains of the blessed one and licking the soles of her feet. He trembled with fear, especially remembering Mary's words when she had said that she had seen no beast during her time in the wilderness. Making the sign of the cross, he trusted that the power of the woman lying there would guard him. The lion began to fawn over the old man, greeting him not only with his movements but also with a plan. Zosimas said to the lion, "Since, beast, the great one entrusted me to bury her remains, and since I am an old man and do not have what I need to dig the pit (for I do not have the necessary digging tool, and I am not able to run back over so far a distance so as to get one), do what you can with your claws so that we may bury the holy one." Immediately, the lion dug a pit with its fore-claws that was large enough to bury the body.

Again the old man washed the feet of the holy one with his tears and entreated her to pray even more now for all people. In the presence of the lion, he covered her body with the earth, which was as naked as it had been before the ragged cloth that Zosimas had thrown her.

Both then departed. The lion turned toward the middle of the desert, retreating like a sheep, while Zosimas returned blessing and praising Christ our God. When he returned to his community, he told the monks everything, concealing nothing that he had heard and seen from the beginning. He told everything piece by piece so that all who heard these great things of God were amazed and with awe and reverent love performed the holy one's memorial. And John, the leader of the monastery, did find certain ones in need of correction, so the words of the holy one did not become hollow and futile. Zosimas came to his end in that monastery at nearly one hundred years of age.

The monks continued to teach orally the story that they had received and presented it to the public as a beneficial example for those who desired to hear. But I have never heard that the narrative had been written down until now. In writing, I have made known what I received. Perhaps others have also written down the life of this holy one, and truly they have done it more magnificently than I, but I have not yet encountered such a thing, and no knowledge of it has come to me. I have written the story according to my ability, and I have not desired to prefer anything but the truth. May God, the one who repays those who take refuge in him with great things, give the reward to those who encounter this narrative, and may God also give that reward to the one who commanded that this be written down, and for their part, may they be judged worthy of the stature and position of the blessed Mary, about whom this narrative was told. With all those who forever are pleasing God by their contemplation and their practice, let us therefore also give praise to God, the one who rules over all the ages, so that God might also deem us worthy of meeting mercy on the day of judgment, in Christ Jesus, to whom belongs all praise, honor, and worship always with the eternal Father, and the holy, beneficent, and life-giving Spirit, now and always and to the ages of the ages. Amen.

LIFE OF MARY OF EGYPT

A Version in Poetry by Amy Frykholm

I.
Chanting psalms at noon,
he saw a shadow

Body, black
Hair, sparse white wool

He ran after her
Tears a river

Until both came to a bed
Where a stream had left a trace.

But how could a torrent
Appear in that land?

Do not despise me,
He called out.

Give me your cloak,
She said.

Are you a ghost? he asked.
I am altogether earth and ashes and flesh, she said.

No spirit here to see.

II.
She told him of her desires
And of the desert
Through which the years had taken her.

She told him to come back
With the Holy Supper
And put it in her mouth.

He came with figs and dates
With soaked lentils
With bread and wine.

She walked across the water to meet him.
She kissed him
With the kiss of love on his mouth.

He fell to his knees
And begged her to pray
for the church, for the empire, for him.

But he did not hold for long
She who would not be held.

III.
When he came again
To the streambed

He saw her body
Pointing east.

He saw a lion
Licking the soles of her feet.

On the sand, he saw
Her name: Mary.

NOTES

PREFACE

4 *I am the whore and the holy one* . . . George W. MacRae, trans., "The Thunder, Perfect Mind," Gnostic Society Library, Nag Hammadi Library, accessed February 16, 2021, http://gnosis.org/naghamm/thunder.html.

9 *. . . as told to St. Sophronius* . . . There are not many versions of Mary's story available either in ancient texts or in English translation. The three most important versions are the following:

    1. The one found in the *Patrologia Graeca* attributed to St. Sophronius, *Patrologia Graeca* 87:3697–726, which is the one used for the translation found in the appendix of this book and the one used for Maria Kouli's translation in Alice-Mary Talbot, ed., *Holy Women of Byzantium: Ten Saints' Lives in English Translation* (Washington, DC: Dumbarton Oaks Research Library and Collection, 2006), 65–94.

    2. The Latin text, translated by Paul the deacon from the Greek of Sophronius in the *Patrologiae Latina*, which is translated by Benedicta Ward in her *Harlots of the Desert*. This text is found in Cistercian Studies 106 (Kalamazoo, MI: Cistercian Publications, 1987), 35–56.

    3. The one created by Andrew of Crete for the Great Canon. This is the version that many Orthodox Christians hear read during the third week of Lent every year and thus the reason that many Orthodox Christians feel an intimate connection with Mary of Egypt, while she has been largely forgotten by the rest of the world.

A fourth version of Mary's story that is important in Western Christianity comes from *The Golden Legend*, a collection of stories of saints that was popular in the Middle Ages. That version of Mary's story led to tellings and retellings, with many embellishments in vernacular languages throughout Europe. See Jacobus de Voragine, *The Golden Legend: Readings of the Saints*, trans. William Granger Ryan (Princeton, NJ: Princeton University Press, 2012). There are also scraps of stories in other ancient documents—for example, *The Lives of the Desert Fathers*—that pick up on similar themes of former prostitutes hiding in the desert as holy people. Some scholars see these as direct antecedents to Sophronius's telling. See Norman Russell, trans., *The Lives of the Desert Fathers* (Yonkers, NY: St. Vladimir's Press, 1981).

9 *...a desert-dwelling patriarch...* Sophronius, the author of the *Life of Mary of Egypt*, traveled all over the ancient Christian world with another monk named John Moschos. Together they gathered stories from monks in the monasteries from Rome to Jordan. John Moschos wrote a book detailing these stories called *The Spiritual Meadow*, trans. John Wortley (Collegeville, MN: Liturgical Press, 2008), which is one of the strangest books I've ever read—part fairy tale, part argument, part chronicle. It is full of somewhat grim humor and what appear to be jokes that are not quite translatable into English. Moschos dedicated this book to Sophronius: "to inform your love, my child." When Moschos died in Rome, Sophronius took his body back to St. Theodosius near Bethlehem, his home monastery. At a late age, Sophronius became the patriarch of Jerusalem. In 636, Sophronius turned the keys of Jerusalem over to Arab invaders in a move to spare the lives of Jerusalem's citizens. He died soon after.

My objections to Sophronius largely came from his treatment of Mary's sexuality. I found it hard to see past his depiction of her to a sympathetic understanding of the woman behind it. In other of his writings, I saw a person who anathematized everyone who disagreed with him about even the slightest matter. His patriarchal letter contains an unusually long list of people that Sophronius would choose to throw out of the church, if allowed.

NOTES

Historian Susan Holman helped me toward a more sympathetic understanding of Sophronius as she pointed to his sense of humor and the way that he elevated a woman for the edification of his fellow monks. In *Crisis of Empire*, Phil Booth also points out that Sophronius's unwillingness to consent to compromises forged by his peers was not stubbornness and fundamentalism but dissent. The emperor wanted to resolve such conflicts so that he could assert his power over the entire territory. Sophronius was not willing to go along. Booth, *Crisis of Empire: Doctrine and Dissent at the End of Late Antiquity* (Berkeley: University of California Press, 2017).

9   *. . . the realities a twelve-year-old girl might have faced in her society . . .* Rosemary Ruether describes the lives of girls and women and why they might have found the asceticism of Christianity appealing: "Girls were married at twelve or thirteen or even earlier to husbands who might be forty years their senior and who had been chosen to cement the political and business ties of the family. Shifting family alliances governed marriages and remarriages and women had little to say in the matter. Unhappy marriages, early pregnancies, being shut out of the larger world of experience and education: these must have helped dispose many women to embrace the new alternative offered by the Church." "Mothers of the Church: Ascetic Women in the Late Patristic Age," in *Women of Spirit: Female Leaders in the Jewish and Christian Tradition*, ed. Rosemary Ruether and Eleanor McLaughlin (Eugene, OR: Wipf and Stock, 1998), 73.

    Aline Rousselle notes the extremely young ages at which girls were forced into intercourse in order to "open up" passages for menstruation. *Porneia: On Desire and the Body in Antiquity*, trans. Felicia Pheasant (Eugene, OR: Wipf and Stock, 1988), 93.

10   *She is a myth . . .* In searching for the historicity of Mary of Egypt, I took a clue from Dostoevsky. As he wrote about the holy man Tikhon, whom he wanted to describe for his readers, he said, "I am not going to create. I am only going to portray a real Tikhon whom long ago, with deep delight, I received into my heart." Quoted in Edith Wyschogrod, *Saints*

and Postmodernism: Revisioning Moral Philosophy (Chicago: University of Chicago Press, 1990), 3.

Lynda Coon sees Mary's story as one fabricated from "paradox and inversion." *Sacred Fictions: Holy Women and Hagiography in Late Antiquity* (Philadelphia: University of Pennsylvania Press, 1997), xiv. But this is not a forgone conclusion of the scholarship. Much of feminist scholarship about late ancient women points out that all historical reconstruction of women's history is "highly tentative" in its nature, as Bernadette Brooten puts it. "The work of women's history," she writes, "must be based upon historical imagination. . . . Woman represents a crack in the system." "Early Christian Women in Their Cultural Context: Issues of Method in Historical Reconstruction," in *Feminist Perspectives on Biblical Scholarship*, ed. Adela Yarbro Collins (Chico: Scholars Press, 1985), 67–68.

12   *". . . it makes its excessive demands in ways that are socially disruptive and destabilizing . . ."* David Jasper, *The Sacred Desert: Religion, Literature, Arts and Culture* (Oxford: Blackwell, 2004), 58.

12   *". . . we know she belongs to us and we to her . . ."* Clarissa Pinkola Estés, *Women Who Run with the Wolves* (New York: Ballantine Books, 1992), 7.

12   *Bewilderment . . .* Fanny Howe, "Bewilderment," Piper Center for Creative Writing, Arizona State University, accessed October 7, 2020, https://tinyurl.com/y4hm7xwz.

FIND THE ROOT

32   *. . . did not displace the river as the center of spiritual and physical life . . .* Of the many accounts of the Christianization of Egypt, I've most appreciated the work of historian David Frankfurter. He has recently documented the fundamentally bricolage nature of early Egyptian Christianity: "Christianity in Egypt in the fifth, sixth, and seventh centuries," Frankfurter writes, "amounted to a framework within which mothers and scribes, artisans and holy men, priests and herdsmen experimented with diverse kinds

of religious materials and traditions." By focusing on local practices and women's contributions, Frankfurter suggests an early Egyptian Christianity that involved "gradual, creative assemblage." They sought to claim "the magic without which life couldn't proceed" in their own way, combining old and new. This is how I imagine Mary's early family life: steeped in these Egyptian traditions that are also merging with and shaping her family's Christianity. Like much of the late ancient world, patronage and belonging were as important as religious identity. *Christianizing Egypt* (Princeton, NJ: Princeton University Press, 2017), 3.

34   *...she didn't leave much of herself behind...* I could see the history of Christianity in Nubia on display at the ruin of the Monastery of St. Simeon, which was built in the seventh century, in the earliest part of Nubia's conversion to Christianity. The monastery functioned until the twelfth century, when it was destroyed by the forces of Saladin. Nubians did not convert to Islam until the twelfth century, unlike the rest of Egypt. So this monastery, in its heyday, was an outpost between civilizations. It was not only on the border between Christianity and traditional religion but on the border between Christianity and Islam and between the desert and the lusher regions of the Nile. It wasn't so much hidden in the desert as it was standing with a foothold in each world. The ruins are remarkably extensive, including a bakery, a stable, several chapels, living quarters, and guest quarters. I had always had an image of a small, fragile Christianity defending itself against Muslim or Arab or Persian or Bedouin invaders, but the Monastery of St. Simeon gave me a different view. There the Christians lit up their towers so that Muslim guests could find them as they were crossing the desert on their way to Mecca. See Gawdat Gabra and Hany N. Takla, *Christianity and Monasticism in Aswan and Nubia* (Cairo: American University in Cairo Press, 2016).

Climb to the High Place

38   ...*deepens their understanding of spiritual life*... In *Sacred Fictions*, Lynda Coon maps out many of the relationships between Paul and Anthony's story and Mary of Egypt's: the search for a holier life, the need to go deeper into the desert, the discovery of a sacred place, the telling of a tale, the request made by the holy person, the burial that involves the presence of lions. She points out that we think of particularity as authentic, but this was not the case for ancient storytellers. For them, the very redundancy, the repetition of familiar motifs, made the story true.

38   *None of the resonances of sex and repentance are present in Anthony and Paul's story*... Geoffrey Galt Harpham gives an erotic reading of the encounter between Paul and Anthony in "Asceticism and the Compensations of Art," in *Asceticism*, ed. Vincent L. Wimbush and Richard Valantasis (New York: Oxford University Press, 1995), 357–68.

40   ...*the rapid growth of Christian monasticism around the time of Anthony*... The phrase "the desert becomes a city" comes from the first account of Anthony, written by St. Athanasius of Alexandria. An English translation by Robert Gregg can be found in *Athanasius: The Life of Antony and the Letter to Marcellinus* (Mahwah, NJ: Paulist Press, 1980).

40   *She had not been remembered in liturgy here*... Coptic Christians use the Liturgy of St. Basil the Great from the fourth century and the Liturgy of St. Mark from the first century. Russian and Greek Orthodox Christians use later versions of Basil's liturgy and include the Great Canon of St. Andrew of Crete, a liturgy for Lent that includes Mary's story. This canon was created in the monasteries of Palestine.

40   ...*this name of the Universal Mother in all three major Abrahamic religions*... On the complexity of the name Mary: Miriam, in the Jewish tradition, was the sister of Moses and therefore the mother of the Jewish religion, since she saved Moses from the Nile when the Hebrews were just being shaped as a people. She shares a name with Mary, who in the Christian tradition was the mother of Jesus and became the Queen of Heaven.

Miryam, Mother of Jesus, in Islam, was the only woman to have an entire book of the Qur'an dedicated to her. And both Christians and Muslims share a pilgrim's path that reflects holy sites where the Holy Family stayed during its flight into Egypt. All of these women under one name created a significant amount of confusion for me on my journey. In my own notes, I had started to call Mary the Mother of God "Mary M.O.G." and Mary of Egypt "M.O.E." But as I talked to people in Egypt, they always and only pointed me to Mary M.O.G.

Sift through the Sand

48 ... *open to experience and open to the heart's whisperings* ... See Georgia Frank, *The Memory of the Eyes* (Berkeley: University of California Press, 2000), 70.

49 "... *live in doorways* ..." The poorest of the prostitutes in the late ancient world were said to practice their trade in doorways and archways. The word *fornicate* comes from the Latin word for "archway." Sarah Pomeroy, *Goddesses, Whores, Wives, and Slaves: Women in Classical Antiquity* (New York: Schocken Books, 1975), 202.

50 ... *Kom el-Dikka had been a center for performances* ... Our most detailed description about life as an Alexandrian actress comes from a text written to impugn the empress Theodora, who was an actress before she converted to Christianity and married Justinian, who was emperor from 527 to 565. Procopius, a political rival, claimed that Theodora and her sisters were trained to perform sex acts on men from the time that they were very small. Procopius describes parties where Theodora might have been hired to have sex with as many men as were at the gathering. He suggests that she was "frequently pregnant" but used abortifacients to avoid having children. In one of the most disturbing and vivid scenes of his account, he describes Theodora performing onstage by having grain sprinkled across her naked body. Geese were then released to descend on her and pick the grains off of her for the entertainment of the crowd. It is disturbing reading and doesn't

make the contemporary reader feel anything but sympathy and even horror for Theodora. See Procopius, *The Secret History*, trans. Richard Atwater (New York: Cosimo Classics, 2007).

52   ... *away from what you need to flee* ... We must be careful not to romanticize the role or the life of prostitutes in this society—or in our own. Prostitution was the profession of women who lacked families, dowries, or inheritance. Some were the daughters of the very poor who had been "lured by pimps." Others were captives from a young age. Parents sometimes sold their daughters. The literature mentions prostitutes being paid in copper coins, the coins that had the least value. They frequently had to beg as well as engage in the sex trade and died young of poor diet and disease. Carolyn Connor, *Women of Byzantium* (New Haven: Yale University Press, 2004), 80–83.

53   ***Both scholars read Mary as a "sex radical" who commands her own pleasure and takes her own path*** ... Virginia Burrus, *The Sex Lives of the Saints: An Erotics of Ancient Hagiography* (Philadelphia: University of Pennsylvania Press, 2004), 147; and Patricia Cox Miller, "Is There a Harlot in This Text? Asceticism and the Grotesque," *Journal of Medieval and Early Modern Studies* 33, no. 3 (2003): 419–35.

54   ... *cautionary tales with troubling outcomes* ... Historian Averil Cameron comments helpfully on the Christian tradition's focus on desire: "We can begin to see now how it is that early Christian discourse attaches so much importance to the concept of desire, eros, for it is desire which effects unification between human and divine, as between male and female, and which unites the world of man with that of the angels, and it is desire again which impels God to create the world, as it is desire which leads human souls to aspire to reach the higher beings on the hierarchy." She also notes that women played a special role in Christian discourse of desire that had very little to do with their own experiences. "Early Christianity and the Discourse of Female Desire," in *Women in Ancient Societies: "An Illusion of the Night,"* ed. Léonie J. Archer, Susan Fischler, and Maria Wyke (New York: Routledge, 1994), 164–65.

56   *Jerome* . . . Quoted in E. D. Hunt, *Holy Land Pilgrimage in the Later Roman Empire AD 312–460* (Oxford: Clarendon, 2002), 100.

57   "*. . . passions lurk . . .*" Historian Peter Brown describes the way that pilgrimages especially broke down barriers between the sexes. Women were "available to the public gaze" in ways that were not true in daily life. Pilgrimage, Brown says, was a "heady elixir." *The Cult of Saints: Its Rise and Function in Latin Christianity* (Chicago: University of Chicago Press, 1981), 43. Pilgrimage was also a leveling force between men and women. Carolyn Connor explains that it was an "option open to all," and so it "exemplified the Christian model of equality before God." Connor, *Women of Byzantium*, 30.

57   "*. . . pious devotion . . .*" Hunt, *Holy Land Pilgrimage*, 68.

57   *. . . the feeling we are supposed to laugh* . . . Trying to understand why and how Mary assigns blame for her particular circumstances, I found some help by looking at desert spirituality more broadly. John Chryssavgis writes that "assuming responsibility for one's life and doing something about it, is the beginning of a truly creative and meaningful life." Demonology of the desert, says Chryssavgis, involves not having control over one's own thoughts and actions. *In the Heart of the Desert* (Bloomington, IN: World Wisdom, 2008), 37.

Another thing that might help explain why Mary so thoroughly blames herself for what happens on the boat is that in the late ancient Christian world, temptation is always the responsibility of the tempting party—that is, it is always the fault of the woman. We do see this tradition continuing today when women who are harassed or abused or even raped are blamed for being immodest or when women are accused—in evangelical Christianity, for example—of causing men to have certain kinds of thoughts. Gillian Cloke, *This Female Man of God* (London: Routledge, 1995), 212.

58   "*. . . the fragrance of the wild soul . . .*" Estés, *Women Who Run*, 21.

BE ASTONISHED

63   *...from Alexandria to the Monastery of St. Anthony*... Monks and pilgrims traveled both by boat and by a road that went along the Mediterranean coast. This was the first road in the area to be completed by the Romans (to suppress revolt by the Jews in the first century). The distance from Alexandria to Jerusalem is only two hundred miles, about two-thirds the distance from Alexandria to the monasteries of Upper Egypt. "Since it was quicker and easier to get to Jerusalem from the capital of Egypt than to many parts of Egypt itself," John Binns writes, "it is not surprising that the highway was well used by monks and pilgrims." Binns, *Ascetics and Ambassadors of Christ* (Oxford: Clarendon, 1996), 158.

66   *... they have been doing this for many centuries ...* The first documented Christian pilgrimage is that of the empress Helena, mother of Constantine, who visited the Holy Land in search of Christian sites early in the fourth century. The first known person to follow in her footsteps was the Bordeaux pilgrim in 333. The next century saw tremendous growth in both pilgrimage and monastery building. Jerusalem went from being a city of soldiers to being a city of pilgrims and monks—and these two were not always distinguishable from each other. Binns, *Ascetics and Ambassadors*, 84.

67   *... Peter Brown ...* See Brown, *Cult of Saints*.

69   *... hundreds of years before ...* What scholars call the Cult of the Virgin Mary developed over the fifth century and into the sixth. This cult combined an elevated public image with the more usual "private and personal role of mother." The first icon of Mary was "found" by the empress Eudokia between 443 and 461 and was said to have been made by St. Luke in Jerusalem in the first century. Judith Herrin, *Unrivaled Influence: Women and Empire in Byzantium* (Princeton, NJ: Princeton University Press, 2013), 185. Other scholars associate the growth of the Cult of Mary with the accompanying images with the goddess Isis as an empress on a throne, acting as a guardian or protectress. See Thomas F. Mathews and Norman

Muller, "Isis and Mary in Early Icons," in *Images of the Mother of God*, ed. Maria Vassilaki (Burlington, VT: Ashgate, 2005), 3–12.

70 *". . . the rest of her life as a hermit . . ."* The website I stumbled upon was Pat McCarthy, "Chapel of Mary of Egypt." See the Holy Land, accessed September 15, 2018, https://www.seetheholyland.net/church-of-the-holy -Sepulcher-chapels/ (link no longer extant).

74 *". . . it needs to be looked into . . ."* Estés, *Women Who Run*, 53.

Cross the Threshold

91 *". . . evidence of that transformation . . ."* Coon, *Sacred Fictions*, 87.

92 *Jerome . . .* Quoted in Lionel Casson, *Travel in the Ancient World* (Baltimore: Johns Hopkins University Press, 1994), 329.

93 *Augustine of Hippo . . .* Quoted in Margaret Miles, *Practicing Christianity: Critical Perspectives for an Embodied Spirituality* (Eugene, OR: Wipf and Stock, 1988), 96.

Open the Door

96 *". . . somewhere in the imagination . . ."* Frank, *Memory of the Eyes*, 1.

99 *". . . gush forth fountains of tears . . ."* From the beginning, I had wondered what to make of Zosimas's constant weeping. Tears, it turns out, play an important role in the Christian desert tradition, which might be why Zosimas does so much crying—and might have something to do with my own tears. Desert spirituality developed what was called the "gift of tears" or the "grace of tears" as a marker of transformation. Kallistos Ware writes that tears are an outward expression of an inward reality, an "enigmatic intersection between body and soul," that lead to the "spiritualization of the senses." Isaac the Syrian said, "Tears mark the boundary between the bodily and the spiritual state. . . . The fruits of the inner self begin only with the shedding of tears. When you reach this place of tears, then know that your spirit

has come out from the prison of this world, and has set its foot upon the path that leads towards the new age. Your spirit begins at this moment to breathe the wonderful air that is there, and it starts to shed tears." Quoted in Kallistos Ware, "'An Obscure Matter': The Mystery of Tears in Orthodox Spirituality," in *Holy Tears*, ed. Kimberley Christine Patton and John Stratton Hawley (Princeton, NJ: Princeton University Press, 2005), 245–58.

Get Lost

110 "*. . . modern means of transportation . . .*" Victor Turner, *Dramas, Fields, and Metaphors* (Ithaca, NY: Cornell University Press, 1974), 225.

110 "*. . . driven deep . . .*" Quoted in Jasper, *Sacred Desert*, 21.

113 *. . . more rarefied than marriage . . .* Teresa Shaw, "Practical, Theoretical, and Cultural Tracings in Late Ancient Asceticism," in *Asceticism*, ed. Wimbush and Valantasis, 79.

Go into the Deeper Desert

121 *. . . the created world in a more elemental way . . .* Kallistos Ware, "The Way of the Ascetics: Negative or Affirmative?," in *Asceticism*, ed. Wimbush and Valantasis, 7.

121 *. . . toward extreme personal regulation . . .* Averil Cameron, "Ascetic Closure and the End of Antiquity," in *Asceticism*, ed. Wimbush and Valantasis, 149.

121 "*. . . as the desert itself . . .*" Burrus, *Sex Lives of the Saints*, 147.

122 "*. . . the only work we have to do . . .*" Estés, *Women Who Run*, 37–38.

Melt

134 "*The church where she stopped is long gone . . .*" Yizhar Hirschfield, *The Judean Desert Monasteries in the Byzantine Period* (New Haven: Yale University Press, 1992), 62.

134   *... that officially ended in 1994...* Just weeks after I visited the site, the Israeli government and a British NGO finished clearing land mines from the area, and we may now gradually be able to see through excavation what historian John Binns describes as a "connected network of monasteries clustered close to the river" on both sides. Binns, *Ascetics and Ambassadors*, 52.

BE WILD

143   *... with the testimony of local people ...* Mohammed Waheeb, *The Discovery of Site of St. Mary of Egypt* (Amman, Jordan: self-pub., 2004), 29.

150   *"... a huge wave over me ..."* Mary attributes this light to the care and guidance of the *Theotokos*. Estés offers an interesting perspective on the *Theotokos* in Mary's story. The *Theotokos* might be understood as "a listener who guides, suggests, and urges vibrant life in the inner and outer worlds." A Wild Woman herself, she "supports the inner and outer life no matter what." She is "both friend and mother to all those who have lost their way, all those who need a learning, all those who have a riddle to solve, all those out in the forest or the desert wandering and searching." *Women Who Run*, 8–9.

FOR FURTHER READING

Binns, John. *Ascetics and Ambassadors of Christ: The Monasteries of Palestine 314–631*. Oxford: Clarendon, 1996.

Brown, Peter R. L. *The Body and Society: Men, Women, and Sexual Renunciation in Early Christianity*. New York: Columbia University Press, 1988.

————. *The Cult of Saints: Its Rise and Function in Latin Christianity*. Chicago: University of Chicago Press, 1981.

Burrus, Virginia, ed. *Late Ancient Christianity*. Minneapolis: Fortress, 2005.

————. *The Sex Lives of the Saints: An Erotics of Ancient Hagiography*. Philadelphia: University of Pennsylvania Press, 2004.

Cameron, Averil. "Early Christianity and the Discourse of Female Desire." In *Women in Ancient Societies: "An Illusion of the Night,"* edited by Léonie J. Archer, Susan Fischler, and Maria Wyke, 152–168. New York: Routledge, 1994.

Cameron, Averil, and Amélie Kuhrt, eds. *Images of Women in Antiquity*. Detroit: Wayne State University Press, 1985.

Caner, Daniel. *History and Hagiography from the Late Antique Sinai*. Liverpool: Liverpool University Press, 2010.

Chitty, Derwas James. *The Desert a City: An Introduction to the Study of Egyptian and Palestinian Monasticism under the Christian Empire*. New York: St. Vladimir's Seminary Press, 1966.

Chryssavgis, John. *In the Heart of the Desert: The Spirituality of the Desert Fathers and Mothers*. Bloomington, IN: World Wisdom, 2008.

Clark, Gillian. *Women in Late Antiquity: Pagan and Christian Lifestyles*. Oxford: Oxford University Press, 1993.

Cloke, Gillian. *This Female Man of God: Women and Spiritual Power in the Patristic Age, AD 350–450*. London: Routledge, 1995.

Connor, Carolyn L. *Women of Byzantium*. New Haven: Yale University Press, 2004.

Coon, Lynda. *Sacred Fictions: Holy Women and Hagiography in Late Antiquity.* Philadelphia: University of Pennsylvania Press, 1997.

Coon, Lynda, Katharine J. Haldane, and Elisabeth W. Sommer, eds. *That Gentle Strength: Historical Perspectives on Women in Christianity.* Charlottesville: University of Virginia Press, 1990.

Elm, Susannah. *"Virgins of God": The Making of Asceticism in Late Antiquity.* Oxford: Clarendon, 1994.

Estés, Clarissa Pinkola. *Women Who Run with the Wolves: Myths and Stories of the Wild Woman Archetype.* New York: Ballantine Books, 1992.

Frank, Georgia. *The Memory of the Eyes: Pilgrims to Living Saints.* Berkeley: University of California Press, 2000.

Frankfurter, David. *Christianizing Egypt: Syncretism and Local Worlds in Late Ancient Christianity.* Princeton, NJ: Princeton University Press, 2017.

Gabra, Gawdat, and Hany N. Takla, eds. *Christianity and Monasticism in Aswan and Nubia.* Cairo: American University in Cairo Press, 2016.

Green, Mary E. *Eyes to See: The Redemptive Purpose of Icons.* New York: Morehouse, 2014.

Harmless, William S. J. *Desert Christians: An Introduction to the Literature of Early Monasticism.* Oxford: Oxford University Press, 2004.

Herren, Judith. "In Search of Byzantine Women." In *Images of Women in Antiquity,* edited by Averil Cameron and Amélie Kuhrt, 167–190. Detroit: Wayne State University Press, 1985.

Hirschfield, Yizhar. *The Judean Desert Monasteries in the Byzantine Period.* New Haven: Yale University Press, 1992.

Hunt, E. D. *Holy Land Pilgrimage in the Later Roman Empire AD 312–460.* Oxford: Clarendon, 2002.

Jasper, David. *The Sacred Desert: Religion, Literature, Arts and Culture.* Oxford: Blackwell, 2004.

Miles, Margaret. *Carnal Knowing: Female Nakedness and Religious Knowing in the Christian West.* Eugene, OR: Wipf and Stock, 2006.

———. *Practicing Christianity: Critical Perspectives of an Embodied Spirituality.* New York: Crossroad, 1988.

Moschos, John. *The Spiritual Meadow*. Translated by John Wortley. Collegeville, MN: Liturgical Press, 2008.

Patton, Kimberley Christine, and John Stratton Hawley, eds. *Holy Tears: Weeping and the Religious Imagination*. Princeton, NJ: Princeton University Press, 2005.

Pomeroy, Sarah. *Goddesses, Whores, Wives, and Slaves: Women in Classical Antiquity*. New York: Schocken Books, 1975.

Rubin, Miri. *Mother of God: A History of the Virgin Mary*. New Haven: Yale University Press, 2009.

Ruether, Rosemary. "Mothers of the Church: Ascetic Women in the Late Patristic Age." In *Women of Spirit: Female Leaders in the Jewish and Christian Traditions*, edited by Rosemary Ruether and Eleanor McLaughlin, 71–98. Eugene, OR: Wipf and Stock, 1998.

Talbot, Alice-Mary, ed. *Holy Women of Byzantium: Ten Saints' Lives in English Translation*. Washington, DC: Dumbarton Oaks Research Library and Collection, 2006.

Turner, Victor. *Dramas, Fields and Metaphors*. Ithaca, NY: Cornell University Press, 1974.

Turner, Victor, and Edith Turner. *Image and Pilgrimage*. New York: Columbia University Press, 1978.

Vassilaki, Maria, ed. *Images of the Mother of God: Perceptions of the Theotokos in Byzantium*. Burlington, VT: Ashgate, 2005.

Waheeb, Mohammed. *The Discovery of Site of Mary of Egypt*. Amman, Jordan: Self-published, 2004.

Ward, Benedicta. *Harlots of the Desert: A Study of Repentance in Early Monastic Sources*. Cistercian Studies 106. Kalamazoo, MI: Cistercian Publications, 1987.

Wilkinson, John, trans. *Egeria's Travels*. Oxford: Aris and Phillips, 1999.

Wimbush, Vincent L., and Richard Valantasis, eds. *Asceticism*. New York: Oxford University Press, 1995.

Wyschogrod, Edith. *Saints and Postmodernism: Revisioning Moral Philosophy*. Chicago: University of Chicago Press, 1990.